BRITISH GEOLOGICAL SURVEY

A BRANDON

CONTRIBUTORS

*Stratigraphy and structure*
A A Jackson, M G Sumbler,
P J Strange, B A Hains and
W J Barclay

*Geophysics*
M J Arthur

*Stratigraphy and sedimentology*
A C Morton

*Petrography*
G E Strong

*Palaeontology*
D E White

# Geology of the country between Hereford and Leominster

Memoir for 1:50 000 geological sheet 198
(England and Wales)

LONDON: HER MAJESTY'S STATIONERY OFFICE    1989

© *Crown copyright 1989*

*First published 1989*

ISBN 0 11 884427 X

*Bibliographical reference*

BRANDON, A. 1989.   Geology of the country between Hereford and Leominster.   *Memoir of the British Geological Survey*, Sheet 198 (England and Wales).

*Author*

A Brandon, BSc, PhD
*British Geological Survey, Keyworth*

*Contributors*

M J Arthur, BSc, MSc, DIC; W J Barclay, BSc;
B A Hains, BSc, PhD; A A Jackson, BSc, PhD;
A C Morton, MA; P J Strange, BSc;
G E Strong, BSc; M G Sumbler, MA;
D E White, MSc, PhD
*British Geological Survey, Keyworth*

*Other publications of the Survey dealing with this district and adjoining districts*

BOOKS

*Memoirs*
Geology of the country around Droitwich, Abberley and Kidderminster, Sheet 182, 1962 (reprinted 1979)
Geology of the country around Tewkesbury, Sheet 216, in press

*British Regional Geology*
The Welsh Borderland (3rd edition), 1971

MAPS

*1:625 000*
**Great Britain (South Sheet)**
Solid geology (3rd edition), 1979
Quaternary geology, 1977
Bouguer anomaly, 1986
Aeromagnetic anomaly, 1965
Hydrogeology, 1977

*1:250 000*
**Mid Wales and Marches Sheet (52°N 04°W)**
Solid geology, in press
Aeromagnetic anomaly, 1980
Bouguer gravity anomaly, 1986

*1:50 000*
Sheet 182   Droitwich, Solid and Drift, 1976
Sheet 198   Hereford, Solid and Drift, in press
Sheet 216   Tewkesbury, Solid and Drift, in press

*1:25 000*
Parts of SO 47, 57   Leintwardine – Ludlow, Solid, 1973

*1:10 000*
Parts of sheets SO 52 NE, SE and 62 NW, SW   Ross-on-Wye Special Sheet, 1980

Printed in the United Kingdom for HMSO

Dd 240427  C10  8/89  3385/2  16268

# Geology of the country between Hereford and Leominster

The predominantly rural district described in this memoir lies within the wide tract of continental Lower Old Red Sandstone rocks stretching from the English Midlands to South Wales. The rocks of the district were deposited during a period of about 25 million years, spanning the Siluro-Devonian boundary. In the south-east, at Shucknall Hill and the northern margin of the Woolhope Dome, there are small inliers of marine Ludlow rocks. These are shallow shelf calcareous siltstones and nodular limestones with a rich benthonic fauna, on which the Lower Old Red Sandstone rests conformably.

The Lower Old Red Sandstone succession displays an upward change of facies, from marginal marine to molasse fluviatile, brought about during the early stages of the Caledonian Orogeny. At the base, the Rushall Formation is a sequence of shaly mudstones and sandstones, with sparse marine faunas in the lowest beds, giving way to restricted marine ostracods, eurypterids, fish and plants in higher beds. The overlying Raglan Mudstone, forming the low-lying land of much of the area, was laid down on the extensive coastal plain of the Anglo-Welsh basin, which was subject to brief marine incursions. The St Maughans Formation, a more proximal fluviatile facies with rhythmical alternations of sandstones, intraformational conglomerates and mudstones, forms the higher ground of the Bromyard plateau in the north-east. Repeated pedogenic limestone horizons (calcretes) within the red beds of these two thick younger formations testify to the aridity of the climate; ostracoderm fish and plants are the commonest fossils encountered in the channel sandstones and conglomerates.

During the late Quaternary the area witnessed two extensive glaciations. The oldest deposits, of probable Anglian age, occur only as remnants beyond the limits of the Devensian glaciation, whose deposits cover most of the western half of the region. River terraces along the Lugg valley date from the interval between the two glaciations. Solifluction deposits are numerous in the area not covered by the Devensian glaciation. Later Quaternary deposits are mainly alluvium and colluvium.

Sections in the memoir deal with the tectonic history and the relatively few mineral deposits; the reference list incorporates a bibliography on the geology of the district.

**Frontispiece**   Looking north from The Slip [5926 3980] in Aymestry Limestone across the hop fields of the Frome Valley, underlain by Raglan Mudstone, head and gravels, to the faulted, wooded Ludlow inlier of Shucknall Hill. The Bromyard plateau of St Maughans Formation occurs in the distance (A13880)

# CONTENTS

TABLES

FIGURES

## PLATES

# PREFACE

The district covered by the Hereford (198) Sheet of the 1:50 000 geological map of England and Wales was originally surveyed on the one-inch scale as parts of Old Series sheets 43 NW by J Phillips and T E James, published in 1845; 43 NE by J Phillips and H H Howell, published in 1845 (revised 1855); and 55 SW by W T Aveline, A R Selwyn, J Phillips and H H Howell, published in 1853 (revised 1855). Geological explanations were not published to accompany these sheets though an account of the Ludlow strata by J Phillips appeared in 1848.

Systematic fieldwork by Drs B A Hains and A Brandon, supported by the Department of the Environment, began around Hereford City in 1977. Dr Brandon extended the mapping and was later joined by Dr A A Jackson and Messrs P J Strange, M G Sumbler and W J Barclay. The mapping of the 1:50 000 sheet was completed in 1983. The 1:10 000 maps and accompanying Open File Reports are listed by surveyor on p.viii. A 1:50 000 Solid and Drift edition of the map is published; this account describes that map.

Fossil fish were identified by Dr P L Forey and Miss V T Young of the British Museum (Natural History). Silurian invertebrates were identified by Dr D E White and Mr D E Butler. The petrography of the sedimentary rocks was described by Mr G E Strong and the geophysics of the district by Mr M J Arthur, both of whom have contributed Open File Reports (see p.viii). A resistivity investigation of the sand and gravel deposits was undertaken by Messrs B Cannell and M R Clarke. The photographs (Appendix) were taken by Messrs C J Jeffery and E R Collins, and the cartography is by Mr C G Murray. Keyboarding was by Mrs C Humber and typesetting by Mrs J B A Evans. The Memoir was edited by Messrs J E Wright, W B Evans, E G Smith and M G Sumbler.

Grateful acknowledgement is made to numerous organisations and individuals, including landowners, quarry operators, consulting engineers and public and local authorities, for generous help during the survey.

F G Larminie, OBE
*Director*

*British Geological Survey*
*Keyworth*
*Nottingham NG12 5GG*

1 March 1989

# DATA HELD BY BGS

## GEOLOGICAL MAPS AT 1:10 000

Complete cover for the district is obtainable as dye-line maps except for part of the southern margin (i.e. parts of sheets SO 33 NE, SO 43 NW, SO 53 NE and SO 63 NW). The surveyors were A Brandon (AB), A A Jackson (AAJ), M G Sumbler (MGS), P J Strange (PJS), B A Hains (BAH), W J Barclay (WJB) and B S P Moorlock (BSPM).

| | | | |
|---|---|---|---|
| SO 34 SE | Preston on Wye (E part) | AAJ | 1987 |
| SO 34 NE | Staunton on Wye (E part) | AAJ | 1987 |
| SO 35 SE | Sarnsfield (E part) | AAJ | 1987 |
| SO 35 NE | Pembridge (E part) | AAJ | 1987 |
| SO 43 NE | Hereford City SW | AB | 1979 |
| SO 44 SW | Kenchester | AB | 1986 |
| SO 44 SE | Hereford City NW | AB | 1979 |
| SO 44 NW | Mansell Lacy | AAJ | 1988 |
| SO 44 NE | Wellington | AAJ | 1986 |
| SO 45 SW | Dilwyn | AAJ | 1983 |
| SO 45 SE | Dinmore | MGS | 1983 |
| SO 45 NW | Eardisland | AAJ | 1983 |
| SO 45 NE | Leominster | MGS | 1983 |
| SO 53 NW | Hereford City SE | BAH | 1979 |
| SO 54 SW | Hereford City NE | AB,BAH | 1986 |
| SO 54 SE | Bartestree | AB | 1984 |
| SO 54 NW | Marden | AB | 1985 |
| SO 54 NE | Preston Wynne | AB | 1987 |
| SO 55 SW | Bodenham | AB | 1984 |
| SO 55 SE | Pencombe | AB | 1984 |
| SO 55 NW | Stoke Prior | AB | 1984 |
| SO 55 NE | Docklow | AB | 1984 |
| SO 63 NE | Little Marcle | BSPM,AB | 1988 |
| SO 64 SW | Ashperton | AB | 1984 |
| SO 64 SE | Bosbury | AB | 1987 |
| SO 64 NW | Much Cowarne | PJS | 1983 |
| SO 64 NE | Bishop's Frome | PJS | 1983 |
| SO 65 SW | Little Cowarne | MGS | 1984 |
| SO 65 SE | Stanford Bishop | PJS | 1984 |
| SO 65 NW | Bredenbury | MGS | 1984 |
| SO 65 NE | Tedstone Delamere | WJB,AAJ | 1984 |

## LAND SURVEY OPEN FILE REPORTS

Complete cover as for 1:10 000 maps, in two series.
Authors' names abbreviated as for maps.
*Geological notes and local details for 1:10 000 sheets*
SO 34 SE & NE, SO 35 SE & NE (E parts)

| | | |
|---|---|---|
| Preston on Wye to Pembridge | AAJ | 1984 |

SO 43 NE, SO 44 SE, SO 53 NW, SO 54 SW

| | | |
|---|---|---|
| Hereford City | AB,BAH | 1981 |
| SO 44 NW Mansell Lacy | AAJ | 1982 |
| SO 44 NE Wellington | AAJ | 1982 |

| | | | |
|---|---|---|---|
| SO 44 SW | Kenchester | AB | 1982 |
| SO 45 NW | Eardisland | AAJ | 1983 |
| SO 45 NE | Leominster | MGS | 1983 |
| SO 45 SW | Dilwyn | AAJ | 1983 |
| SO 45 SE | Dinmore | MGS | 1983 |
| SO 54 NW | Marden | AB | 1982 |
| SO 54 NE | Preston Wynne | AB | 1982 |
| SO 54 SE, SO 64 SW | | | |
| | Bartestree & Ashperton | AB | 1982 |
| SO 55 NW & SW | | | |
| | Stoke Prior & Bodenham | AB | 1987 |
| SO 55 NE & SE | | | |
| | Docklow & Pencombe | AB | 1987 |
| SO 63 NE | Little Marcle | BSPM | 1984 |
| SO 64 NW | Much Cowarne | PJS | 1982 |
| SO 64 NE | Bishop's Frome | PJS | 1982 |
| SO 64 SE | Bosbury | AB | 1982 |
| SO 65 NW | Bredenbury | MGS | 1985 |
| SO 65 SW | Little Cowarne | MGS | 1985 |
| SO 65 NE | Tedstone Delamere | WJB,AAJ | 1984 |
| SO 65 SE | Stanford Bishop | PJS | 1984 |

*Geological reports for the DoE: Land Use Planning*

| | | |
|---|---|---|
| Quaternary deposits of Sheet SO 44 | AAJ | 1982 |
| Quaternary deposits of Sheet SO 54 | AB | 1982 |
| Quaternary deposits of Sheet SO 64 | PJS,AB | 1982 |
| Geology of Sheet SO 45 | AAJ,MGS | 1983 |
| Geology of Sheet SO 55 | AB | 1984 |
| Geology of Sheet SO 65 | MGS | 1984 |

## SPECIALIST UNITS' OPEN FILE AND INTERNAL REPORTS

**Applied Geophysics Unit**
No. 122  Investigations of geophysical anomalies in the Herefordshire area of the Welsh Borderland. M J Arthur  1982

**Petrology Unit**
No. 147  Raglan Marl specimens from Herefordshire. G E Strong  1979

No. 169  Petrography of some Lower Old Red Sandstone specimens from the Bullinghope and Dinedor areas, Herefordshire.  G E Strong  1979.

No. 228  Petrology of Lower Old Red Sandstone specimens of the Wootton area, Herefordshire. G E Strong  1982.

No. 236  Petrography of Raglan Marl specimens from Herefordshire.  G E Strong  1983.

No. 245  Petrography of Old Red Sandstone specimens from Herefordshire.  G E Strong  1983.

No. 268  Petrographical notes on Raglan Marl and St Maughan's Group (L. Old Red Sandstone) rocks from localities in Hereford and Worcester. G E Strong 1984.

**Industrial Mineral Assessment Unit**
No. 83/1  The investigation of shallow drift deposits in the Leominster, Herefordshire area, using the off-set Wenner shallow resistivity system.  M R Clarke and B Cannell  1983.

**Stratigraphy and Sedimentology Research Group**
No. 88/8 Stratigraphic relationships and provenance of Lower Old Red Sandstone samples from Herefordshire assessed by heavy mineral analysis. A C Morton 1988

## PHOTOGRAPHS

An album of coloured prints is available for consultation. It illustrates the full range of the geology of the district. The photographs are available also as black and white prints and as 35 mm colour slides (*see* Appendix).

## ROCK SAMPLES

A full range of thin sections of the sandstones of the Lower Old Red Sandstone, as well as other rocks, has been cut. They have been used in describing the geology and are available with the registered specimens for consultation on request.

## BOREHOLE DATA

The results of shallow drilling are available for consultation. There are no deep boreholes in the district.

In the first instance, enquiries about the geology of the district should be directed to BGS headquarters at Keyworth, Nottingham NG12 5GG: Telephone Plumtree (06077) 6111.

x

# ONE

# Introduction

This memoir describes the geology of the country covered by 1:50 000 Geological Sheet 198 (Hereford) shown in Figures 1 and 2. The general topography is depicted on the front cover. The survey was conducted between 1977 and 1983, and detailed reports on the geology of 1:10 000 geological sheets are available. Detailed accounts of the Quaternary geology of four combined 1:10 000 geological sheets, (i.e. a National Grid square of 100 sq km), with special emphasis on potential resources of sand and gravel, have also been prepared for the Department of the Environment who partly funded the original survey. These geological sheets with corresponding Open File Reports and authors are tabulated on

p.viii, which also lists reports on the petrography of the rocks by G E Strong and on investigations of the geophysical anomalies of the Hereford area by M J Arthur.

The district forms a large part of the so-called Plain of Hereford which is underlain by the Lower Old Red Sandstone. The western and southern parts of the district are predominantly lowland, underlain by the easily weathered Raglan Mudstone Formation and cut by the broad valleys of the rivers Arrow, Lugg, Frome and Wye. The north-eastern part, between Leominster and Bromyard, is an undulating plateau up to 253 m above OD, made up of resistant sandstones and mudstones of the overlying St Maughans Forma-

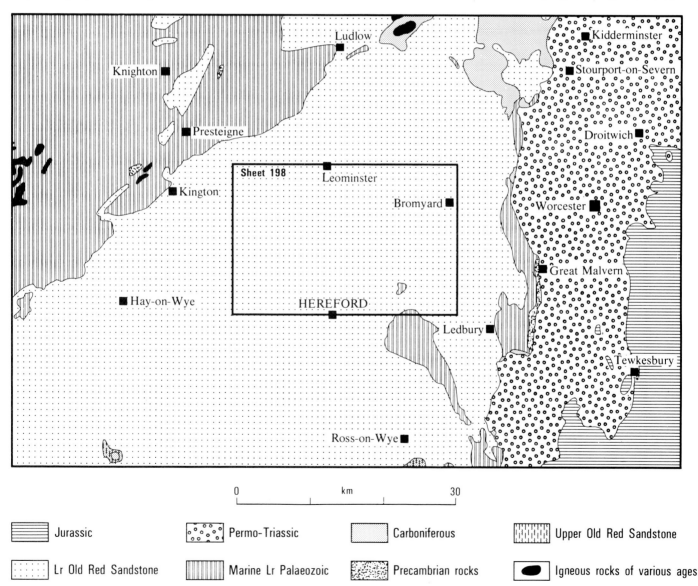

Jurassic · Permo-Triassic · Carboniferous · Upper Old Red Sandstone · Lr Old Red Sandstone · Marine Lr Palaeozoic · Precambrian rocks · Igneous rocks of various ages

**Figure 1**  Regional setting of the Hereford geological sheet

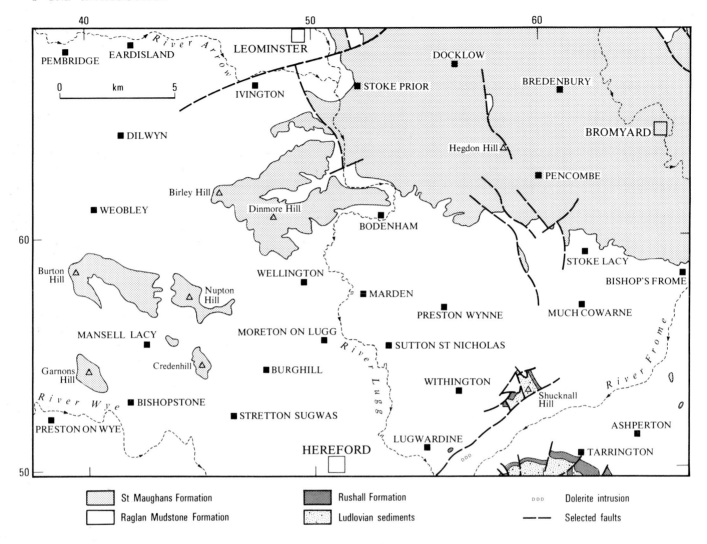

**Figure 2**   Generalised solid geology of the area

tion. Small outliers of this formation comprise tabular hills in the south-west, such as Garnons Hill [400 445][1] and Credenhill [450 445]. The largest is the buttress of Burton Hill [395 487], the highest point in the district at 294 m above OD. Towards the south-east, Shucknall Hill [595 435] (Frontispiece) and the rising slopes of the Woolhope Hills are elevated areas composed of faulted inliers of harder, and slightly older, Ludlow strata.

Much of the low ground west of the River Lugg is covered by glacial till and moraine together with fluvioglacial gravels, the products of the last (Devensian) glaciation of the district by upland ice from the west.

Most of the land is privately owned and permission should be obtained for access to areas away from public footpaths. Furthermore, visitors to localities should always conform to the Code of Conduct for geology, published by the Geologist' Association, which is reproduced in part at the end of this memoir.

The lithological and stratigraphical divisions of the rocks found in the district are shown in the table inside the front cover.

1 Figures in square brackets are National Grid references within the 100 km square SO.

TWO

# Silurian: Ludlow

## INTRODUCTION

The successions in the Woolhope Dome (Squirrell and Tucker, 1960) and the Collington Borehole [646 610] (Department of Energy, 1978; Penn, 1987) indicate that the area is underlain at depth by up to 1200 m of Llandovery, Wenlock and Ludlow strata resting on Precambrian basement. Only the highest Ludlow strata occur at the surface.

They crop out in the northern part of the Woolhope Dome south of Tarrington [618 407], and there are smaller inliers at Shucknall Hill [595 434] (Frontispiece) and Hagley [561 409]. The rocks are calcareous siltstones and nodular limestones, and comprise the Lower Ludlow Siltstone, Aymestry Limestone and Upper Ludlow Siltstone formations. Table 1 gives their thicknesses, illustrates the biostratigraphical classification of the Woolhope–Shucknall area (Squirrell and Tucker, 1960), and gives a comparision with the type area at Ludlow (Holland and others, 1959, 1963).

Gardiner (1927) divided the Ludlow rocks of the Woolhope Inlier into the Lower Ludlow Shales, Aymestry Limestone and Upper Ludlow Beds, following the divisions established by Murchison (1834a). Squirrell and Tucker (1960) erected new divisions for these strata, defined mainly on their faunal assemblages, but controlled to some extent by sedimentary facies. In the present survey it proved more practical to retain the earlier tripartite subdivision of the Ludlow rocks with some updating of the names (e.g. the Lower Ludlow Shales are here called the Lower Ludlow Siltstone Formation). The formations are somewhat diachronous (see for example Phipps and Reeve, 1967, p.352).

The rocks were deposited in a warm, shallow shelf sea near the south-eastern margin of the Iapetus Ocean. The district then lay at about latitude 15° South (Smith and others, 1981), and the sea nurtured a diverse shelly benthonic fauna dominated by brachiopods. The broad palaeontology is outlined in Figure 3, which gives the stratigraphical ranges of the more common and characteristic fossils, several of which are illustrated in Figure 4. A more detailed account of the palaeontology is provided by Squirrell and Tucker (1960). Ludlow faunal associations and facies are discussed by Holland and Lawson, 1963; Calef and Hancock, 1974; Lawson, 1975, and Watkins, 1979.

**Table 1**  Ludlow stratigraphy

| LITHOSTRATIGRAPHICAL FORMATIONS | BIOSTRATIGRAPHICAL CLASSIFICATION | | CHRONOSTRATIGRAPHICAL STAGES |
|---|---|---|---|
| | WOOLHOPE–SHUCKNALL AREA Squirrell and Tucker, 1960 | LUDLOW AREA Holland, Lawson and Walmsley, 1959; 1963 | |
| Upper Ludlow Siltstone (ULu) (85 m) | Upper Perton Beds (UPB) (14 m) | Upper Whitcliffe Beds | Ludfordian |
| | Lower Perton Beds (LPB) (27 m) | Lower Whitcliffe Beds | |
| | Upper Bodenham Beds (UBB) (4.5 m) | Upper Leintwardine Beds | |
| | Lower Bodenham Beds (LBB) (40 m) | Lower Leintwardine Beds | |
| Aymestry Limestone (AL) (15 m) | Upper Sleaves Oak Beds (USOB) (28 m) | Upper Bringewood Beds | Gorstian |
| Lower Ludlow Siltstone (LLu) (285 m) | Lower Sleaves Oak Beds (LSOB) (84 m) | Lower Bringewood Beds | |
| | Upper Wootton Beds (UWB) (97 m) | Upper Elton Beds | |
| | Lower Wootton Beds (LWB) (91 m) | Middle Elton Beds Lower Elton Beds | |

**Figure 3**   Simplified range chart of selected Ludlow fossils from the Woolhope Inlier and Shucknall Hill. (Modified by D E White after Squirrel and Tucker (1960)). (Authors of species are given in the index)

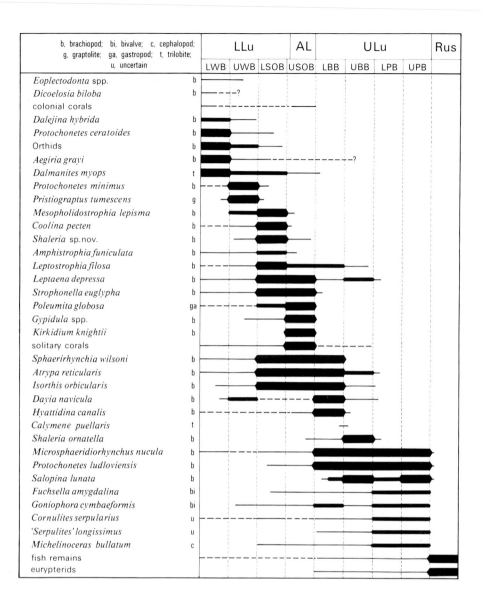

| b, brachiopod;  bi, bivalve;  c, cephalopod; g, graptolite;  ga, gastropod;  t, trilobite; u, uncertain | | LLu | | | | AL | ULu | | | | Rus |
|---|---|---|---|---|---|---|---|---|---|---|---|
| | | LWB | UWB | LSOB | USOB | LBB | UBB | LPB | UPB | | |
| Eoplectodonta spp. | b | | | | | | | | | | |
| Dicoelosia biloba | b | | ? | | | | | | | | |
| colonial corals | | | | | | | | | | | |
| Dalejina hybrida | b | | | | | | | | | | |
| Protochonetes ceratoides | b | | | | | | | | | | |
| Orthids | b | | | | | | | | | | |
| Aegiria grayi | b | | | | | | | ? | | | |
| Dalmanites myops | t | | | | | | | | | | |
| Protochonetes minimus | b | | | | | | | | | | |
| Pristiograptus tumescens | g | | | | | | | | | | |
| Mesopholidostrophia lepisma | b | | | | | | | | | | |
| Coolina pecten | b | | | | | | | | | | |
| Shaleria sp.nov. | b | | | | | | | | | | |
| Amphistrophia funiculata | b | | | | | | | | | | |
| Leptostrophia filosa | b | | | | | | | | | | |
| Leptaena depressa | b | | | | | | | | | | |
| Strophonella euglypha | b | | | | | | | | | | |
| Poleumita globosa | ga | | | | | | | | | | |
| Gypidula spp. | b | | | | | | | | | | |
| Kirkidium knightii | b | | | | | | | | | | |
| solitary corals | | | | | | | | | | | |
| Sphaerirhynchia wilsoni | b | | | | | | | | | | |
| Atrypa reticularis | b | | | | | | | | | | |
| Isorthis orbicularis | b | | | | | | | | | | |
| Dayia navicula | b | | | | | | | | | | |
| Hyattidina canalis | b | | | | | | | | | | |
| Calymene puellaris | t | | | | | | | | | | |
| Shaleria ornatella | b | | | | | | | | | | |
| Microsphaeridiorhynchus nucula | b | | | | | | | | | | |
| Protochonetes ludloviensis | b | | | | | | | | | | |
| Salopina lunata | b | | | | | | | | | | |
| Fuchsella amygdalina | bi | | | | | | | | | | |
| Goniophora cymbaeformis | bi | | | | | | | | | | |
| Cornulites serpularius | u | | | | | | | | | | |
| 'Serpulites' longissimus | u | | | | | | | | | | |
| Michelinoceras bullatum | c | | | | | | | | | | |
| fish remains | | | | | | | | | | | |
| eurypterids | | | | | | | | | | | |

## LOWER LUDLOW SILTSTONE FORMATION

The full thickness of the formation in the northern part of the Woolhope area is about 285 m, though only the upper strata crop out within the district, on Shucknall Hill and also as two small patches near Cockshoot [606 397] and around the southern side of Tower Hill [592 397] in the Woolhope Inlier. Because of the structural complexities at Shucknall the thickness represented by the outcrop is uncertain but is probably about 97 m. When fresh the beds consist of tough, poorly fissile, olive-grey, highly calcareous siltstones with numerous hard, grey, fine-grained, limestone nodules about 10 to 20 cm across. In weathered sections the siltstones are decalcified, becoming brown and platy. The highest 13 m are well displayed in the core of a tight anticline in a large quarry [5914 4305] on Shucknall Hill (Plate 1). On faunal grounds Squirrell and Tucker (1982, p.11) placed only the lowest metre of these beds within the Lower Sleaves Oak Beds (Table 1), the remainder falling into the lower part of the Upper Sleaves Oak Beds, which are lithologically, but

not faunally, distinct from the Aymestry Limestone proper (Tucker, personal communication, 1985). Many of the nodules there show a dichotomous form and are localised on burrows of *Thalassinoides* (Mohamad, 1981; Squirrell and Tucker, 1982, p.13).

## AYMESTRY LIMESTONE FORMATION

This formation is about 15 m thick at outcrop and forms a strong topographical feature. It consist of massive beds about a metre thick, comprising roughly equal proportions of calcareous siltstone and harder fine-grained limestone. The latter form nodules which in places coalesce into seams 5 to 7 cm thick. Both lithologies are blue-grey and extremely tough when fresh, as for example in the working Perton Quarry, where the rock is not obviously nodular. In the older quarries, however, the siltstones are decalcified and yellow-brown giving the rock a distinctive appearance. Fossils are common, particularly corals and large brachio-

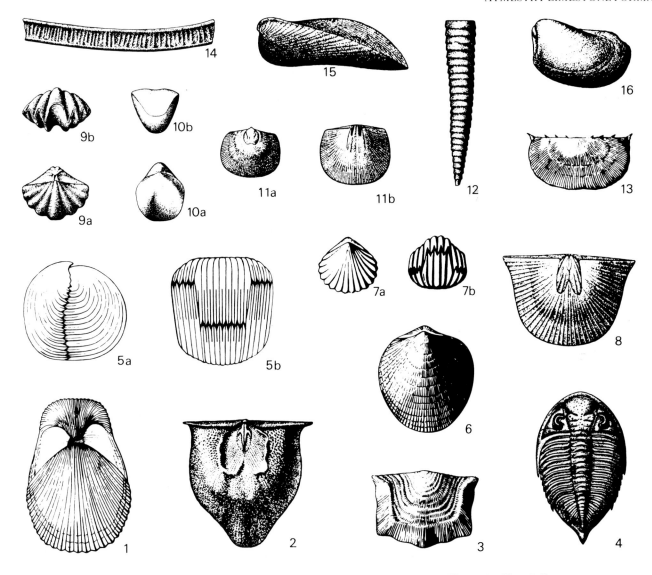

**Figure 4** Selected Ludlow fossils: their stratigraphical ranges are shown in Figure 3. *Howellella elegans* ranges throughout the Ludlow Series.

1 *Kirkidium knightii* (J Sowerby) (× ½). 2 *Strophonella euglypha* (Dalman) (× ¾). 3 *Leptaena depressa* (J de C Sowerby) (× 1). 4 *Dalmanites myops* (König) (× 1). 5a,b *Sphaerirhynchia wilsoni* (J Sowerby) (× 1½). 6 *Atrypa reticularis* (Linnaeus) (× 1). 7a,b *Microsphaeridiorhynchus nucula* (J de C Sowerby) (× 1½). 8 *Shaleria ornatella* (Davidson) (× 1½). 9a,b *Howellella elegans* (Muir-Wood) (× 1½). 10a,b *Dayia navicula* (J de C Sowerby) (× 1½). 11a,b *Salopina lunata* (J de C Sowerby) (× 1½). 12 *Cornulites serpularius* Schlotheim (× ¾). 13 *Protochonetes ludloviensis* (Muir-Wood) (× 1½). 14 *'Serpulites' longissimus* (J de C Sowerby) (× ½). 15 *Goniophora cymbaeformis* (J de C Sowerby) (× 1). 16 *Fuchsella amygdalina* (J de C Sowberby) (× 1).

pods. Many of the nodules are localised on *Omphiomorpha* and *Lingula* burrows (Mohamad, 1981; Squirrell and Tucker, 1982, p.13).

Thin layers of incompetent, greyish brown, unctuous, bentonitic clay have been reported at several levels (Squirrell and Tucker, 1960; Mohamad, 1981, p.28), but are rarely seen. They act as slip-planes for rock-slides, such as the one that took place in 1979 at Perton Quarry (p.44). The bentonite seams have been worked on Shucknall Hill (p.45).

The limestone was formerly much used for road aggregate, and the numerous small pits on Shucknall Hill provide partial weathered sections [e.g. 5914 4390]. The full thickness of the formation is exposed in a large pit on Shucknall Hill [5915 4306], where the lowest beds are weathered to a brown rottenstone with nodules and veins of calcite. They overlie sharply but conformably a 2 m-thick bed without nodules at the top of the Lower Ludlow Siltstone. Some 2 m of more shaly beds in the basal part of the

**Plate 1** The steep easterly limb of the Shucknall Anticline in the Lower Ludlow Siltstone Formation, Shucknall Hill Quarry [5914 4305] (A13872)

overlying formation are virtually inaccessible at the top of the north-east face of the quarry. The uppermost 5 m of the Aymestry Limestone, overlain by 3 m of more shaly siltstone at the base of the Upper Ludlow Siltstone, are also exposed in a small quarry [5882 4275] and an adjacent track. Large brachiopods such as *Strophonella euglypha* are absent from the higher shaly beds, which contain *Atrypa reticularis* and *Isorthis orbicularis*. Much of the formation is also exposed at Perton Quarry [595 399], although the unstable face makes examination dangerous. The characteristic features and fauna are more obvious in degraded sections such as the nearby 8.5 m backscarp to The Slip [5927 3980]. The tumbled blocks here are particularly good places to search for fossils, and yield numerous specimens of *Kirkidium knightii*.

## UPPER LUDLOW SILTSTONE FORMATION

The formation is an estimated 85 m thick around Perton and on Shucknall Hill. The predominant lithology is olive-grey, weakly fissile, flaggy siltstone. Most of the rocks are probably calcareous in the fresh state, but all weathered outcrops are decalcified to some extent. Some levels are crowded with iron-stained external casts of brachiopods; others are apparently barren. Bioturbation of the original sediment accounts for the unbedded character of some of the siltstones. Thin nodular to lenticular beds of grey, argillaceous lime-

stone are common, and contain articulated brachiopod valves. Beds of shelly detrital coquinoid limestone, up to about 10 cm thick, are also present throughout the formation. Intraformational conglomerates of calcareous siltstone and limestone pebbles in a limestone matrix indicate hard grounds in the lowest 14 m (Cherns, 1980), and condensed biotite-rich layers, associated with fish remains, worm tubes, conodonts and comminuted shells, occur at several horizons (Squirrell and Tucker, 1960, pp.148, 150; Tucker, 1960). Beds of grey, hard, platy, calcareous, fine-grained, silty, cross-bedded, generally unfossiliferous sandstone and sandy siltstone occur in the highest 15 m.

Small exposures are numerous on Shucknall Hill and around Perton, Stoke Edith and Tarrington, but extensive sections are uncommon, a ditch exposure along the east side of the Perton Lane [5971 4035 to 5960 4001] being the most continuous (Squirrell and Tucker, 1982, p.13). The lowest 10 m and the transition from the Aymestry Limestone are best exposed at Perton Quarry [595 399] (Watkins, 1979, p.194). Many small pits were opened in the nineteenth century to work the tough siltstone and sandstone for building stone or aggregate and most are still open. Plate 2 shows one such disused quarry [5871 4264] on Shucknall Hill with a section of siltstones containing *Shaleria ornatella*. The highest 1.2 m were formerly exposed in a now infilled pit in the small inlier at Hagley Park [5603 4089] (Strickland, 1852).

**Plate 2** Weakly fissile olive-grey siltstone with limestone nodules belonging to the Upper
Bodenham Beds of the Upper Ludlow Siltstone Formation, small disused quarry [5871 4264] on
Shucknall Hill (A13877)

THREE

# Silurian and Devonian: Lower Old Red Sandstone

## INTRODUCTION

Lower Old Red Sandstone rocks occupy the whole of the district apart from the Ludlow inliers. They comprise in ascending order, the Rushall, Raglan Mudstone and St Maughans formations, which all consist of silty mudstones and sandstones, with pedogenic limestones (calcretes) in the two higher formations. Sandstones are more common in the upper part of the succession.

Figure 5 shows the estimated thicknesses of the formations and gives their stratigraphical relationship to the divisions of the Lower Old Red Sandstone in adjacent areas. The Brownstones Formation, the highest part of the Lower Old Red Sandstone, does not occur in the district, but crops out to the south around Ross on Wye.

The Ludlow Bone Bed, at the base of the Rushall Formation, marks a change from the shallow marine conditions of the Ludlow to the mainly continental conditions of the local Lower Old Red Sandstone. These latter sediments were laid down on a coastal plain largely by rivers draining hot semi-arid areas (Figure 6). Under these conditions, animal life was restricted and rarely preserved; macrofossils are consequently scarce, though regionally in the lower part of the Raglan Mudstone there are thin beds with a restricted fauna of ostracods, bivalves, lingulids, eurypterids and fish, which represent shallow marine or brackish water conditions. Higher in the sequence fossil remains are mainly of ostracodermal fish and plant debris (Table 2 and Figure 8).

## STRATIGRAPHICAL CLASSIFICATION

The history of the nomenclature is complex. The stratigraphy of the Lower Old Red Sandstone in the Anglo-Welsh Basin has been summarised by Allen (1977), and the historical complexities of nomenclature discussed by Allen and Tarlo (1963, p.146) and Bassett and others (1982). The Lower Old Red Sandstone was zoned on the basis of its ostracoderm fish faunas by White (1950a and b), who erected stages based on King's (1925, 1934) stratigraphical divisions for the West Midlands. Such names as 'Downtonian Stage' and 'Dittonian Stage' were used by King largely as lithostratigraphical concepts (White, 1945, p.208), but they were also later given a chronostratigraphical connotation and now have an ambiguous status (Squirrell, 1973). Whitehead and Pocock (1947, p.8) proposed a dual classification in which King's 'Downtonian' and 'Dittonian' referred to the age of the rocks based on fish faunas, and 'Downton Series' and 'Ditton Series', divided at the base of the 'Psammosteus' Limestone, were introduced for the lithological sequence. However, because some beds, e.g. the 'Psammosteus' Limestones (of King, 1925), were demonstrably diachronous with respect to fish zones (White, 1950b), the palaeontological divisions did not match exactly with the lithological divisions. The present account avoids using these ambiguous names, and instead a strict lithostratigraphical system has been adopted, following a scheme originally formulated by Pocock (1940) for the Forest of

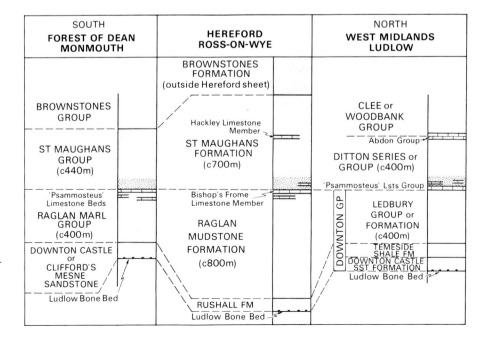

**Figure 5** Terminology of the Lower Old Red Sandstone of the Hereford district and adjoining areas (not to scale; dots mark the incoming of sandy strata of 'Ditton' facies)

Dean and used in other districts such as Monmouth and Newport (Squirrell and Downing, 1969). The names have been adapted to conform with their formational status, thus the Raglan Marl Group becomes the Raglan Mudstone Formation, and the St Maughans Group becomes the St Maughans Formation. The Ross–Tewkesbury Spur motorway section near Ross-on-Wye exposes the most complete section through these formations and has been described in modern terms (Allen and Dineley, 1976); it forms the type section for both formations.

Figure 5 shows the relationships of formations of the Hereford district to the 'groups' and formations of the adjacent areas. The Rushall Formation is synonymous with the Rushall Beds of Squirrell and Tucker (1960), and probably equates with the combined Downton Castle Sandstone and Temeside Shale formations of Ludlow. The term Ledbury Group was originally applied to only a small basal part of the red Downton succession (King, 1925, 1934), but in 1935 was used by Pocock and Whitehead for the entire red 'Downtonian' in the northern areas, and was later applied in this sense to the Hereford–Ross area (Allen, 1977). The boundary between the Raglan Mudstone and St Maughans formations is taken at the top of the main 'Psammosteus' Limestone (the Bishop's Frome Limestone Member of this account), following the practice in southern areas. Workers in the northern areas favoured placing the boundary at the base of that limestone. The limestone is almost continuous across the district, and is only absent locally due to channelling. Minor, apparently impersistent limestones occur below and above the main limestone in southern and northern areas respectively, hence the terms 'Psammosteus' Limestones (King, 1925) and 'Psammosteus' Limestone Group, Beds or phase (Squirrell and Downing, 1969). The concept of a persistent and extensive main limestone is nevertheless generally accepted.

The base of the local (chronostratigraphical) 'Downtonian' was taken by White (1950a and b) at the Ludlow Bone Bed, and he placed the 'Downtonian'–'Dittonian' boundary between his zones of Traquairaspis (Phialaspis) symondsi and Pteraspis (Simopteraspis) leathensis. Clarke (1951; 1952; 1955a and b) demonstrated, from fragmentary fish remains, that the boundary falls roughly 55 m above the main 'Psammosteus' Limestone in the Hereford district. There is also local evidence for the higher 'Dittonian' zone of Rhinopteraspis crouchi in the St Maughans Formation (Table 2). The chronostratigraphical classification has recently been under review, and the position of the Silurian–Devonian boundary, long established at the Ludlow Bone Bed, has been revised upwards to conform with international usage, based on the marine graptolite zones of Central Europe. The redefinition of the Silurian–Devonian boundary has required the erection of a fourth Silurian series above the

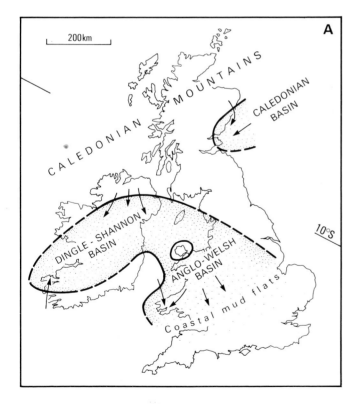 

**Figure 6**   Palaeogeography of Lower Old Red Sandstone times showing sedimentary basins and fluvial dispersal systems, **A** during deposition of Raglan Mudstone Formation and **B** during deposition of St Maughans Formation (after Allen and Crowley, 1983). Approximate palaeolatitude of the times is shown (after Smith and others, 1981)

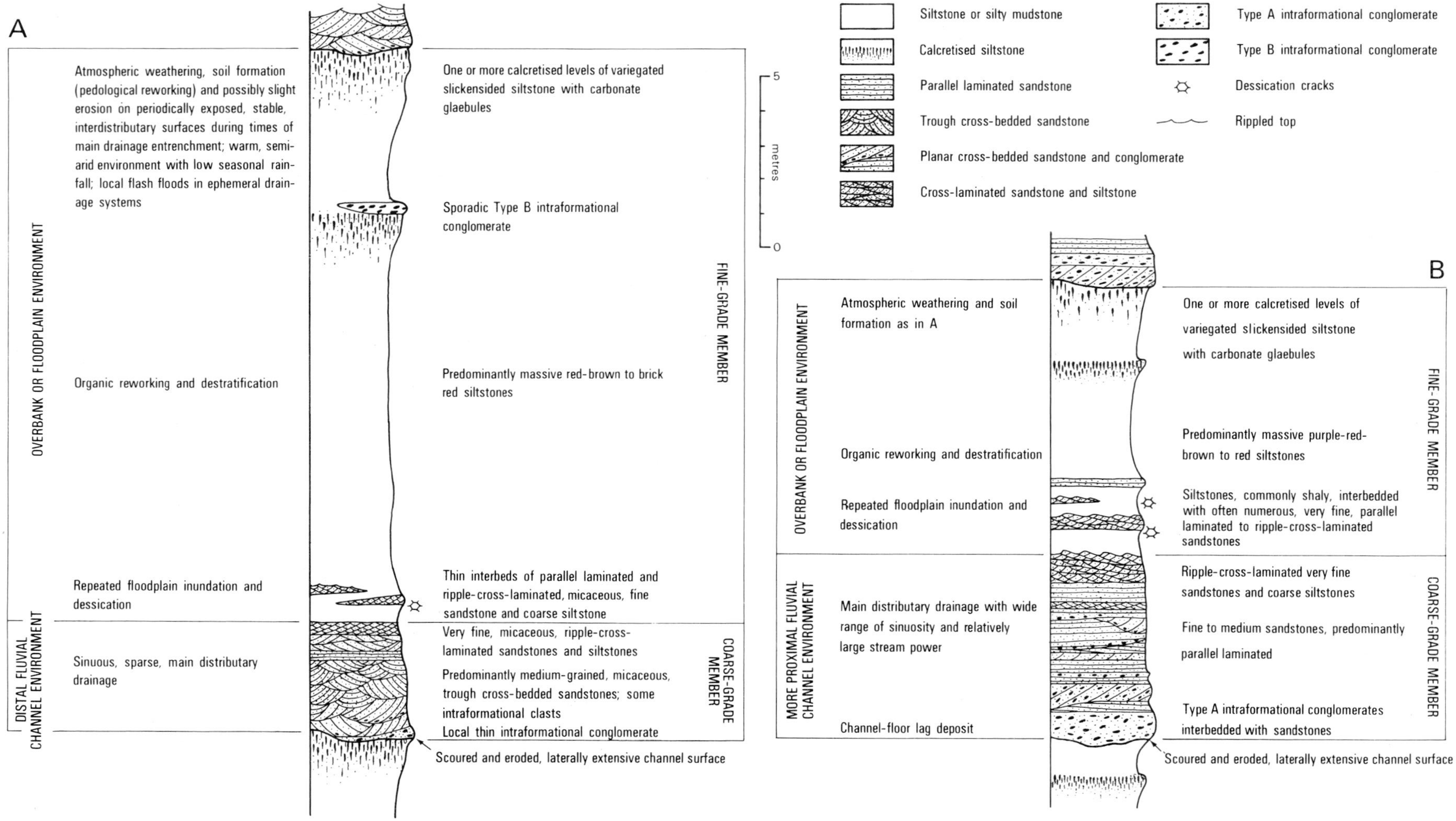

**B**

FINE-GRADE MEMBER

COARSE-GRADE MEMBER

Type A intraformational conglomerate

Type B intraformational conglomerate

Dessication cracks

Rippled top

Siltstone or silty mudstone

Calcretised siltstone

Parallel laminated sandstone

Trough cross-bedded sandstone

Planar cross-bedded sandstone and conglomerate

Cross-laminated sandstone and siltstone

One or more calcretised levels of variegated slickensided siltstone with carbonate glaebules

Predominantly massive purple-red-brown to red siltstones

Siltstones, commonly shaly, interbedded with often numerous, very fine, parallel laminated to ripple-cross-laminated sandstones

Ripple-cross-laminated very fine sandstones and coarse siltstones

Fine to medium sandstones, predominantly parallel laminated

Type A intraformational conglomerates interbedded with sandstones

Scoured and eroded, laterally extensive channel surface

Atmospheric weathering and soil formation as in A

Organic reworking and destratification

Repeated floodplain inundation and dessication

Main distributary drainage with wide range of sinuosity and relatively large stream power

Channel-floor lag deposit

OVERBANK OR FLOODPLAIN ENVIRONMENT

MORE PROXIMAL FLUVIAL CHANNEL ENVIRONMENT

metres

5

0

**A**

FINE-GRADE MEMBER

COARSE-GRADE MEMBER

One or more calcretised levels of variegated slickensided siltstone with carbonate glaebules

Sporadic Type B intraformational conglomerate

Predominantly massive red-brown to brick red siltstones

Thin interbeds of parallel laminated and ripple-cross-laminated, micaceous, fine sandstone and coarse siltstone

Very fine, micaceous, ripple-cross-laminated sandstones and siltstones

Predominantly medium-grained, micaceous, trough cross-bedded sandstones; some intraformational clasts

Local thin intraformational conglomerate

Scoured and eroded, laterally extensive channel surface

Atmospheric weathering, soil formation (pedological reworking) and possibly slight erosion on periodically exposed, stable, interdistributary surfaces during times of main drainage entrenchment; warm, semi-arid environment with low seasonal rainfall; local flash floods in ephemeral drainage systems

Organic reworking and destratification

Repeated floodplain inundation and dessication

Sinuous, sparse, main distributary drainage

OVERBANK OR FLOODPLAIN ENVIRONMENT

DISTAL FLUVIAL CHANNEL ENVIRONMENT

**Figure 7** Idealised cyclothems characterising **A** the main part of the Raglan Mudstone Formation and **B** the St Maughans Formation (after Allen, e.g. 1974b). In each case the thickness of the coarse-grade member has been slightly exaggerated

Ludlow, and in 1985 the name Přídolí Series was chosen (Holland, 1986, p.9). This boundary cannot be recognised in the terrestrial sequence of the Welsh Borders, but it probably lies within the middle or upper part of the Raglan Mudstone Formation (Allen and Williams, 1981, p.27). Thus the Lower Old Red Sandstone, previously considered to be entirely Devonian, is now regarded as Siluro-Devonian in age.

## CONDITIONS OF DEPOSITION

Sedimentological research on the Old Red Sandstone of the Anglo-Welsh basin, notably by J R L Allen, has greatly advanced understanding of the depositional environment. Summaries of the numerous papers are given by Allen (1974c, 1979, 1985), Allen and Williams (1979, 1982) and Williams (1980).

The Old Red Sandstone of the Anglo-Welsh basin accumulated as an off-lapping wedge between the developing 'Caledonide' continent to the north and an expanding ocean to the south (Figure 6). The Rushall Formation is a marginal marine sequence deposited on a prograding sandy shore followed by tidal mud flat deposits. The Ludlow Bone Bed is presumably a lag concentrate or shoal deposit formed during the post-Ludlow marine regression when terrigenous material was in short supply. It rests upon a scoured, and possibly bored, surface of the Upper Ludlow Siltstone.

The Raglan Mudstone and St Maughans formations are characterised by repeated sedimentary cycles that fine upwards (Figure 7), and were formed by rivers migrating across the alluvial plains of the Anglo-Welsh basin. The mainly muddy sediments of the Raglan Mudstone were laid down on an extensive distal fluvial plain or coastal flat. This area, initially subject to marine incursions, was crossed by sinuous, channelled rivers, which scoured and channelled the flat, probably bringing terrigenous sandy detritus from metamorphic sources far to the north-west (Figure 6A). Allen (1974a) has shown that the calcrete-rich pedogenic mudstones or cornstones form part of the normal cycle. They indicate that subaerial exposure and soil formation prevailed periodically. Their presence suggests that the area experienced a relatively hot equatorial climate with low seasonal rainfall. Palaeogeographical reconstructions based on palaeomagnetic data (Smith and others, 1981, pp.78, 82; Livermore and others, 1985, figures 5 and 6) indicate that the area lay in the southern hemisphere within 30° of the Equator (Figure 6). The pedogenic carbonates increased in thickness with time, and thick massive beds, such as those of the Bishop's Frome Limestone, indicate stability between the river channels for periods of probably 10 000 years or more (Allen, 1974a; Leeder, 1975).

In the St Maughans Formation a more proximal and unquestionably fluviatile facies predominated. The formation differs from the Raglan Mudstone mainly in that the coarser-grained sandstone and conglomerate members of the cycles are thicker and more numerous, though fining-upward cycles are maintained. During the deposition of this formation the Anglo-Welsh basin became more restricted (Figure 6B) as a result of uplift caused by granite intrusion at depth (Allen and Crowley, 1983). The basin was denied direct supplies of sediment from distant metamorphic sources, and was fed almost exclusively from sedimentary and volcanic sources of early Palaeozoic age lying much nearer, possibly in and around the Irish Sea. Recycling of an extensive cover of earlier Lower Old Red Sandstone rocks may also have taken place.

## RUSHALL FORMATION

The Rushall Formation crops out only in the south-east of the district, around the Ludlow inliers near Stoke Edith [605 407] and Shucknall Hill [587 433], and in a small inlier at Hagley [561 409]. The rocks were formerly referred to locally as the Downton Sandstone (Strickland, 1852; Stamp, 1923, p.371; Gardiner, 1927) despite there being at least an equal proportion of interbedded mudstone and shale (the 'olive shales' of early workers) within the formation. In the West Midlands the equivalent beds have been divided into a lower Downton Castle Formation (principally sandstones) and an upper Temeside Formation (principally mudstones and shales) (Allen, 1977, pp.42–44), but this distinction cannot be made in the Hereford district. The Rushall Formation is indifferently exposed. Field debris gives the impression that sandstone is the predominant lithology, but the few continuous sections in the northern part of the Woolhope Inlier (e.g. Perton Lane) show that argillaceous beds are important, even low in the formation.

The rocks are interbedded, medium-grained, hard, brown to yellow-brown sandstones, and pale greyish brown, medium brown and pale grey shales, shaly mudstones and siltstones. Individual beds are normally less than 1 m thick. Fossils are generally common (see Figure 8 and Table 2). Comminuted eurypterid remains are abundant in the argillaceous beds in the lower part of the formation, and the old Perton Lane quarry [5971 4035] is renowned for the well-preserved specimens it has yielded (Brodie, 1869, 1871, p.258; Woodward, 1871; Kjellesvig-Waering, 1951). The carbonised alga *Pachytheca*, macerated plant fragments, horny brachiopods, ostracods and fish are also common. *Actinophyllum*, a possible medusoid trace, and the stratigraphically important ostracod *Frostiella groenvalliana* (generally misidentified as *Kloedenia wilkensiana*) are present in the basal beds at Perton; the articulate Ludlow brachiopods *Microsphaeridiorhynchus nucula*, *Protochonetes ludloviensis* and *Salopina lunata* survive into the basal 25 cm of the formation in the Woolhope area (Squirrell and Tucker, 1960, p.51). No complete section is exposed and the lowest beds are the best seen. The basal 5 m exposed at Perton Lane quarry are mostly shales, with two thin sandstones in the basal 0.3 m and three near the top. The thickness is estimated at 15 m, though at Hagley only about 4 m may be present. The lower boundary is everywhere sharp, but the upper boundary is probably transitional. Augering shows that pale grey, brown and dark purple-brown mudstones are common within this transition zone, together with reddish brown mudstones more typical of the Raglan Mudstone.

The Ludlow Bone Bed, at the base of the formation, is not persistent across the district. It was recorded at Hagley Quarry [5603 4089] (Strickland, 1852 and 1853; Stamp, 1923, p.371) as being from a wafer to about 1½ inches thick.

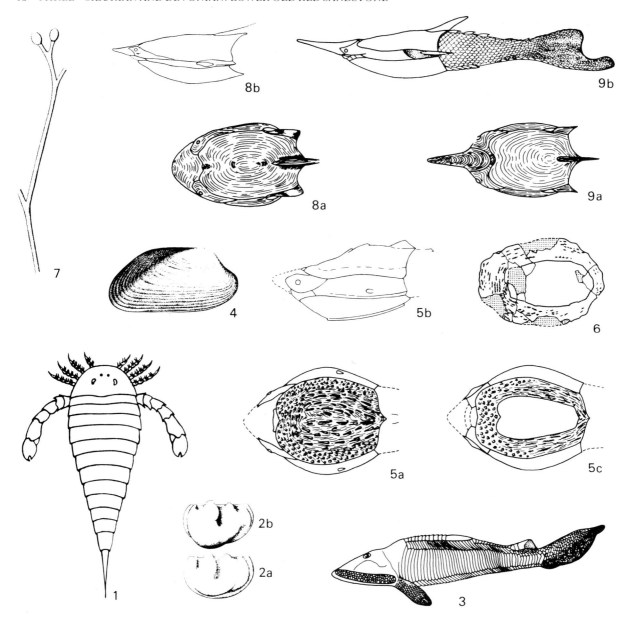

**Figure 8**  Selected Lower Old Red Sandstone fossils.

1   The eurypterid *Eurypterus brodiei* Woodward ( × 1) (as originally reconstructed by Woodward, 1871); Rushall Formation.

2a,b   The ostracod *Frostiella groenvalliana* (Martinsson) ( × 7½), left male and female valves; Rushall Formation.

3   The cephalaspid fish *Hemicyclaspis murchisoni* (Egerton) ( × ⅓); Přídolí.

4   The bivalve *Modiolopsis complanata* (J de C Sowerby) ( × 1); Raglan Mudstone.

5a–c   The pteraspid fish *Traquairaspis (Phialaspis) pococki* White ( × 1), dorsal, lateral and ventral views of head; Raglan Mudstone.

6   The pteraspid fish *Traquairaspis (Phialaspis) symondsi* (Lankester) ( × ²/₅), imperfect ventral head disc; St Maughans Formation.

7   The primitive vascular plant *Cooksonia* sp. ( × ½); Lower Old Red Sandstone.

8a,b   The pteraspid fish *Pteraspis (Simopteraspis) leathensis* White ( × ¾), dorsal and lateral views of head; St Maughans Formation.

9a,b   The pteraspid fish *Rhinopteraspis crouchi* (Lankester) ( × ²/₅), dorsal view of head and lateral view of reconstructed specimen; St Maughans Formation.

**Table 2**   Fossils found in the Lower Old Red Sandstone of the Hereford district

| | Fish zones | | | Locality and reference |
|---|---|---|---|---|
| | *Rhinopteraspis crouchi* | Fish: Head plates of *R. crouchi,* acanthodian spines | | Grendon Bishop [5910 5600] |
| ST MAUGHANS FORMATION (c.700 m) | *Pteraspis (Simopteraspis) leathensis* | Fish: *P. leathensis, Poraspis* cf. *elongata,* cephalaspid shield, acanthodian spines <br> Plants: *Nematothalus* sp., *Cooksonia* sp., *Pachytheca* sp. <br> Millipede: *Kampecaris dinmorensis* | | Birley Hill Quarry [457 522] <br> Garnons Hill [400 445] <br> Dinmore Hill [507 516] <br> (White, 1945; Clarke 1951, 1952, 1955b) |
| | *Traquairaspis (Phialaspis) symondsi* | Fish: *T. symondsi, Tesseraspis tessellata, Oniscolepis* sp., *Ischnacanthus* sp., cephalaspid, acanthodian and '*Onchus*' spines <br> Plants: *Pachytheca* sp., *Parka* sp. | | |
| | | Fish: *Tesseraspis* sp. (1.5 m below Bishop's Frome Limestone) | | Dinmore railway tunnel [5116 5123] |
| RAGLAN MUDSTONE FORMATION (c.800 m) | *Traquairaspis (Phialaspis) pococki* | Fish: '*Onchus*' spine (within 100 m of Bishop's Frome Limestone) | | Dinmore Hill [488 491] (Clarke, 1952) |
| | | Fish: *Kallostrakon?,* '*Onchus*' spines <br> Bivalves: *Modiolopsis complanata* | | Haywood [4828 3587, 4818 3564] (Brandon and Hains, 1981) |
| | | Brachiopod: *Lingula* sp. (c.170 m above base of formation) | | East of Shucknall Hill [6033 4418] |
| RUSHALL FORMATION (c.15 m) | | Brachiopods: *Lingula minima, Protochonetes ludloviensis, Salopina lunata* <br> Fish: *Cyathaspis banksii,* '*Onchus*' spines, *Thelodus parvidens* scales <br> Eurypterids: *Eurypterus brodiei, Hughmilleria banksii, Pterygotus gigas, Salteropterus abbreviatus* <br> Ostracods: *Frostiella groenvalliana;* Plants: *Pachytheca* sp. | | Hagley [5603 4089] (Strickland, 1852, 1853; Stamp, 1923) <br> Perton Lane Quarry [5971 4035] (Kjellesvig-Waering, 1951) |
| Ludlow Bone Bed (up to 4 cm) | | Brachiopods: *Orbiculoidea rugata, Salopina* sp. <br> Fish: '*Onchus*' spines, *Thelodus parvidens* scales | | |

(*marker "55 m" appears to left of Traquairaspis (Phialaspis) symondsi zone*)

It is absent at the Perton Lane quarry (Brodie, 1871, p.259), though Squirrell and Tucker (1960, p.151; 1982, p.13) recognised pockets of bone material within the topmost 'Perton Beds'. It is also absent 100 m to the west [5962 4036], where 0.4 m of hard, brown, medium-grained, thin-bedded sandstone at the base of the Rushall Formation rests sharply on grey, fine-grained sandstones and siltstones of the Upper Ludlow Siltstone. Elsewhere along the northern rim of the Woolhope Inlier and at Shucknall Hill, there is no evidence of the Ludlow Bone Bed. To the south-east of Tarrington, Gardiner (1927, p.516) found a basal conglomerate with fish remains.

## RAGLAN MUDSTONE FORMATION

The Raglan Mudstone Formation forms rock-head in the west and south of the district; west of the River Lugg it is largely covered by glacial deposits. Consisting mainly of mudstones with subordinate sandstones and limestones (calcretes), the rocks have generally not resisted erosion, and there is a lack of good sections. Over most of the area the thickness is estimated at about 800 m. The Collington Borehole [646 610], just outside the district to the north of Bromyard, penetrated about 560 m, but commenced below

the top (Department of Energy, 1978; Tunbridge, 1983, p.327). Geophysical surveys in the west suggest that locally the formation is much thinner (p.25). It is only about 400 m to the south near Ross on Wye (Allen and Dineley, 1976) and Monmouth (Welch and Trotter, 1961), and also to the north in the Clee Hills (Allen, 1974b).

The succession comprises a repetitive sequence of fining-upward cycles of sandstones and mudstones with calcretes (Figure 7A). Coarse-grade and fine-grade members alternate vertically on a scale of metres to tens of metres. Some cycles are incomplete. Generally sandstone forms about ten per cent of the succession.

The top of a thick and mature calcrete, the main 'Psammosteus' Limestone, here named the Bishop's Frome Limestone Member (p.17), has been taken as the top of the formation and is a useful marker band throughout the district and beyond. The formation cannot be subdivided further, and King's (1925, 1934) subdivisions for the West Midlands have not been recognised. The uppermost 100 m of strata are mainly brick-red mudstones with abundant immature calcretes and fewer mappable sandstones than below.

Macrofossils are scarce (Figure 8 and Table 2). Thin beds with a restricted shallow marine to brackish water fauna of ostracods, bivalves (including *Modiolopsis complanata*), lingulids, eurypterids and fish in the lower part of the formation are recorded from comparable levels elsewhere in the Anglo-Welsh Basin (King, 1934, pp.532–535; Allen, 1974b, p.134; Bassett and others, 1982, p.9).

In South Wales coastal sections, Allen and Williams (1978) showed that the formation contains variegated tuffs and siliceous tuffaceous mudstones (porcellanites) up to several metres thick at numerous levels, with a composite 2 to 4 m unit of three graded airfall tuffs (the Townsend Tuff Bed) forming a widespread marker about 100 m below the main 'Psammosteus' Limestone. The tuffs are the product of distant, but powerful, explosive eruptions, the volcanic debris being spread widely over the extensive coastal mud-flats. Allen and Williams record the Townsend Tuff Bed from the Ludlow, Monmouth and Black Mountains (also Clarke, 1951, p.203; Parker and others, 1983) areas and it has recently been located near Bosbury, just east of the district (Brandon, 1988); it is possibly the tuff exposed in the Breinton gorge south of Hereford (Brandon and Hains, 1981, p.8), but it has not been found within the district, though blocks of massive green siliceous porcellanite in the glacial deposits may be derived from it. Smectite is the major clay component of the Townsend Tuff Bed at localities adjacent to the Hereford district and in the Clee Hills area (Merriman, 1988; Parker and others, fig. 4). These locations lie within a zone at the eastern end of the Lower Old Red Sandstone outcrop which was subject to a minimum of diagenetic alteration due to increase in pressure and temperature, since they were buried under a cover of comparatively thin later sediments.

## Sandstones and conglomerates

The coarse-grade members of the sedimentary cycles are mainly sandstones with sharp bases, locally overlying deeply eroded surfaces. They make up about 10 per cent of the formation and are vertically and laterally aggraded deposits laid down by meandering rivers. Their basal few centimetres commonly contain mudstone flakes and calcrete nodules that are locally sufficiently abundant to form thin, highly calcareous conglomerates. These lag deposits commonly contain ostracoderm fish fragments, but they are only a minor facies and are generally neither as thick nor as common as those in the St Maughans Formation.

The sandstones are characteristically medium to coarse grained and exhibit large-scale trough cross-bedding. Upwards they become finer, silty and parallel- or ripple-laminated, and grade fairly rapidly into or interleave with micaceous, laminated sandy siltstones. In contrast to the sandstones of the St Maughans Formation they are conspicuously micaceous, with large muscovite flakes, particularly in their upper parts, making the rocks fissile and flaggy. Some can be split into flexible laminae. Carbonaceous plant fragments are not uncommon, and there are casts of desiccation cracks on the bases of some beds. The sandstones are commonly highly calcareous when fresh and a satin lustre is locally conspicuous. As a consequence of solution of the cement, some of the rocks weather to a very friable condition. Their colour is variable, with pale red-brown and green-grey and various shades of brown predominating. The thickness of the sandstones varies from a few centimetres to several metres; those beds recorded as more than about 5 m thick are probably multiple, or exceptionally deep channel-fills. Beds also vary considerably in thickness laterally, and only exceptionally do sandstones form features for more than two kilometres along the strike. An unusually coarse sandstone, at least 4 m thick and some 300 m above the base of the formation, has a synclinal outcrop about Withington village [562 439]; it contains numerous rounded pebbles of vein-quartz. This and other beds have been extensively quarried for building stone in the past.

Thin sections show the sandstones to be greywackes and subgreywackes composed mostly of detrital quartz, with variable amounts of muscovite, biotite, potassium feldspar, albite-oligoclase and some fine-grained igneous rock fragments. Mudstone pellets and calcrete clasts also occur. Detrital garnet is common, and traces of tourmaline, zircon, sphene, epidote and pyroxene, as well as glauconite and phosphatic fish fragments, are present. Some sandstones are close-packed with little or no early pore-filling cement, but grain-contact welding and pressure-solution contacts are common. Others have a cement of neomorphic calcite spar, commonly poikilotopic. Secondary quartz occurs as cement and grain overgrowths, and authigenic clays (kaolinite, chlorite, and white-mica) are common. Chlorite commonly replaces biotite. Most specimens are slightly iron-stained, particularly those with appreciable biotite and mudstone intraclasts. The sandstones are, therefore, texturally and mineralogically submature to immature. The overall mineral suite, especially the abundance of garnets and large muscovite flakes, is consistent with derivation from the Caledonian metamorphic complexes of north-west Britain, as proposed by Allen (1974b), Simon and Bluck (1982), and Allen and Crowley (1983) (Figure 6A). Heavy mineral analysis on six Hereford sandstones indicates that garnet is dominant (mean 87.9 per cent), epidote is a major component (12 per cent), apatite (5.9 per cent) and tourmaline (5.3 per cent) are less abundant, and rutile (1.8 per cent) and zircon (0.5 per cent) are minor constituents. Staurolite, sphene and chloritoid are rare in some of the sandstones. Palaeocurrent measurements from cross-bedding (Figure 9) confirm that the district was crossed by streams flowing from the north-west quadrant during the deposition of the Raglan Mudstone.

## Mudstones

The mudstone beds are generally several times thicker than the sandstones, and are characteristically blocky or massive, seldom laminated, and are only rarely fissile. They are mainly red-brown to brick-red in colour, and in places contain thin green-grey beds or 'reduction' spots. The mudstones lying directly beneath sandstones have generally been reduced to a green colour for a few centimetres, and a similar colour change is common adjacent to joints. Petrologically the mudstones are siltstones, for the clay fraction forms only 2 to 15 per cent of the detrital grains, but silty mudstone has been used as a field description. Most of the grains consist of fine to coarse quartz silt with a little fine quartz sand and fine white and brown mica flakes. The clay component comprises about 40 to 45 per cent illite, 20 to 40 per cent smectite (including mixed-layer illite/smectite), and 15 to 25 per cent chlorite. Ferric oxides form most of the cement, and impart

**Figure 9** General sediment transport directions during deposition of the Raglan Mudstone and St Maughans Formations, derived from cross-bedding azimuths and parting lineations. Each rose diagram is grouped into 30° classes and the number of field observations, followed by the number of localities, are given in brackets

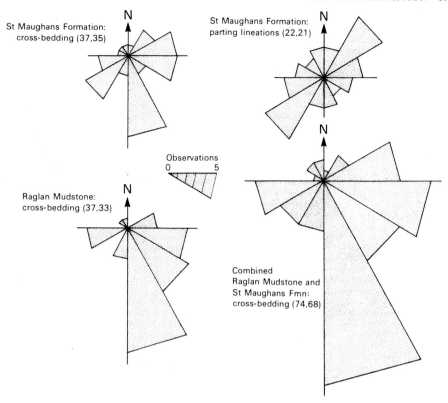

St Maughans Formation: cross-bedding (37,35)

St Maughans Formation: parting lineations (22,21)

Observations
0          5

Raglan Mudstone: cross-bedding (37,33)

Combined Raglan Mudstone and St Maughans Fmn: cross-bedding (74,68)

the characteristic red colour to the rocks. Possible desiccation cracks have been seen in thin section. The mudstones are only weakly calcareous in the fresh state, normally with less than 0.5 per cent $CaCO_3$. Allen and Williams (1982) showed that the massive mudstones were organically or pedologically reworked or destratified while soft. Extensive bioturbation is shown by numerous burrows or root channels.

With an increase in the abundance of large mica flakes, the mudstones develop fissility and pass into or are interbedded with fine-grained, parallel- or ripple-laminated, micaceous silty sandstones, particularly just above the main channel sandstones. Sand-filled mud cracks are characteristic in these interbeds, and point to deposition on repeatedly drowned flood plains (Allen, 1979).

The mudstones commonly contain thin beds of hard intraformational conglomerate, normally less than 0.2 m thick, similar to, but lacking the quartzose sandstone matrix of the main channel lag deposits. Such beds, the Type B conglomerates of Allen and Williams (1979), resulted from local flash floods in minor systems of ephemeral drainage, developed on broad interfluves between the entrenched principal rivers.

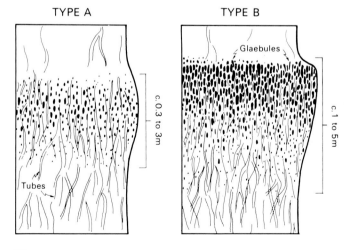

**Figure 10** The two intergrading types of vertical profile encountered in pedogenic carbonate units in the Raglan Mudstone and St Maughans Formations (after Allen, 1974a)

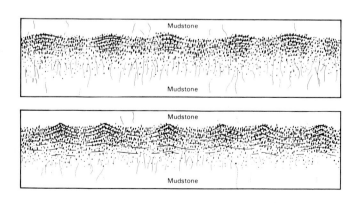

**Figure 11** Schematic vertical profiles through pedogenic carbonate units in the Lower Old Red Sandstone, showing two varieties of pseudoanticline (after Allen, 1974b)

**Plate 3** The Bishop's Frome Limestone in a shallow adit mine [4459 4485], Credenhill.

Note the 'pseudo-anticline' structure and sharp upper boundary to the mature calcrete which is virtually massive in its lower part (A13941)

## Calcretes

The mudstones pass upwards into distinct beds of calcreted mudstone in which the $CaCO_3$ cement content of the matrix increases sharply to over 10 per cent and small irregular nodules or glaebules of fine-grained silty limestone appear, increasing in size and abundance upwards (Figure 10). These nodular beds are the cornstones *senso stricto*, first described by Buckland (1821, p.512) though Murchison (1839) confused the term by including under it the superficially similar conglomerates with detrital calcrete pebbles. In spite of the problem being resolved by M'Cullough (1869, p.8) in the Hereford area, the confusion persisted until recently when Allen (1960) confirmed M'Cullough's views. It is now accepted (Burgess, 1960; Allen, 1974a; Leeder, 1975) that nodular cornstones are calcretes or fossil soil horizons formed in a semiarid environment. The process of calcretisation results from the movement of ground water in the vadose zone, bringing up soluble calcium carbonate from lower levels, and depositing it, as a result of evaporation, close to the ground surface. The glaebules are usually white, cream or pink in colour, though the red colour of the host sediment may be retained. They are associated with, and commonly built around, numerous branching subvertical tubes, several millimetres in diameter and tens of centimetres long, filled with silt or sparry carbonate, which may have been animal burrows or root channels. The glaebules tend to be arranged with subvertical long axes. Slickensided joints are common in the softer host mudstone and are accompanied by carbonate-filled fractures. The calcreted mudstones are highly variegated in tones of purple, green and blue, as well as red. The volume change leads sometimes to the growth of 'pseudo-anticline' structures in which the entire calcreted bed appears to be folded with a fan-like arrangement perpendicular to wave-like fractures (Figure 11; Plate 3). This is probably an expression of polygonally patterned ground. The size and density of the nodules, as well as the overall bed thickness, is a measure of the maturity of a particular soil horizon, or the duration of stability of a particular subaerially exposed area. Many cyclothems include more than one carbonate unit. Calcretes vary from thin blocky red mudstones with sparse nodules (Figure 10, Type A), to highly variegated beds up to several metres thick with a concentration of larger nodules at the top of the profile (Figure 10, Type B; Plates 3 and 4). Calcretes of Type A are predominant in the Raglan Mudstone; those of Type B tend to occur more commonly towards its top. The lower part of a calcrete may, in a few cases, occur partly within a sandstone bed.

At the top of the formation calcrete development was sufficiently prolonged for the nodules (10 cm or more in size) to form more than half of the rock or even almost to replace the discoloured host sediment. The most mature of these calcretes is the main 'Psammosteus' Limestone. The name 'Psammosteus' Limestones was introduced by King (1925, p.385) to refer to a belt of strata in which several limestones occur, corresponding in the Hereford district to the uppermost Raglan Mudstone and lowermost St Maughans formations. 'Psammosteus' is doubly misleading, for not only is the ostracoderm fish *'Psammosteus anglicus'* now referred to

**Plate 4**   Entrance to the adit mine [4459 4485] in the Bishop's Frome Limestone on Credenhill.

The mine occurs at the base of a quarry which exposes the lowest channel sandstone in the local St Maughans Formation succession. This exhibits low angle cross-stratification and rests erosively on variegated calcreted mudstone. The sharp top to the limestone can be seen above the mine entrance (A13942)

two distinct species of *Traquairaspis* (*Phialaspis*), but the fish do not come from the pedogenic limestones but from sandstones and shales associated with them (White, 1945, p.208). The main limestone in the Hereford district is therefore here named the Bishop's Frome Limestone Member. In the district at least one much thinner, and apparently impersistent, limestone occurs about 10 m below the main bed. For instance Clarke (1952, p.225) recorded a thin bed on Dinmore Hill which may be the same as 0.4 m of limestone exposed near Stoke Prior [5145 5632]. This would have been considered to be the lowest limestone of the 'Psammosteus' Limestone Group or 'Psammosteus' Beds by earlier workers. This part of the sequence probably contains a higher frequency of immature calcrete profiles than below, and there may be several profiles in some cyclothems. Allen

(1985, p.95) suggested that the development of the 'Psammosteus' Limestone facies was tectonically controlled, associated as it is with the widespread changes of sediment provenance, depositional style, facies and fauna that occurs at the boundary between the Raglan Mudstone and St Maughans formations.

The Bishop's Frome Limestone Member is generally 2 to 5 m thick, but possibly reaches 8 m locally. The base is transitional with the underlying mudstone, and in the lower parts the mudstone host sediment may form 50 per cent of the rock. The upper boundary is fairly sharp (Figure 10, Type B; Plate 3). The main part of the rubbly bed is composed of large nodules of grey-white limestone set in a sparse variegated mudstone matrix. The nodules become so large and abundant near the top that they coalesce locally to form a massive limestone bed, for example on Credenhill [4459 4485] (formerly mined for building stone—see Plates 3 and 4) and near Stoke Prior [517 565]. The outcrop is generally marked by a line of old lime pits, and good sections may still be found in some of these, for example at Marlbrook [5055 5463] and on Garnons Hill [404 436]. The limestone is probably best exposed in a trackside [6455 4883] at Wootton Farm, Bishop's Frome. Here it is 2.8 m thick, with the transitional base and the top clearly seen. In a few places the main limestone appears to be absent, for example at Hansnett Wood [660 425], where it has probably been channelled away prior to the deposition of an overlying sandstone.

## ST MAUGHANS FORMATION

Like the Raglan Mudstone, the St Maughans Formation consists of mudstones, sandstones and calcretes, but here the sandstones make up 25 to 35 per cent of the sequence and the cycles are generally thinner. The typical St Maughans cycle is illustrated in Figure 7B.

Because of the higher proportion of sandstone, the formation is generally more resistant to erosion than the Raglan Mudstone, and it forms the higher ground in the north-east of the district. Here there are deep stream gulleys with numerous discontinuous sections, the harder beds commonly capping small waterfalls. The formation also forms prominent outliers west of the River Lugg, and there are two small outliers in the south-east at Gains's Hill and Hansnett Wood (Figure 2). In the Bromyard area the thickness is thought to be about 700 m which may be compared with estimates of 630 m at Ross-on-Wye (Allen and Dineley, 1976), 440 m around Monmouth (Welch and Trotter, 1961, p.33) and about 400 m in the Clee Hills (Ball and Dineley, 1961; Allen, 1974b).

No formal subdivision of the formation has been attempted. The lowest few tens of metres contain several thin, apparently discontinuous, strongly developed calcretes (part of King's (1925) 'Psammosteus' Limestones). Discontinuous calcretes probably occur throughout the formation, and a well developed horizon, here named the Hackley Limestone Member, lies 350 to 400 m above the base of the formation in the Bromyard area. This member, with other less mature beds close to it, may correlate with a persistent group of pedogenic concretionary limestones and mudstones at or near the top of the formation around Ross and Monmouth (Allen and Dineley, 1976, p.7; Welch and Trotter, 1961, pp.39, 45, 46), with the Ruperra Limestone of the Newport district (Squirrell and Downing, 1969, p.37), and possibly with the Abdon Limestone of the Clee Hills (Allen, 1974b, p.77). In these areas the limestone 'group' is only a short distance below the sandy beds of the Brownstones Formation and its equivalents. At Bromyard, however, rocks typical of the St Maughans Formation continue for several hundred metres above the Hackley Limestone.

Outside the district, to the south-east of Bromyard, five green siltstone bands, probably lying within the lowest 60 m of the formation, are exposed in a railway cutting at Ammons Hill [700 529] (King, 1934, pp.533–534). They have yielded a restricted marine fauna (Reed, 1934, p.571). The lowest two bands occur only a few metres above a mature calcrete which is probably the Bishop's Frome Limestone; they have yielded the ostracod *Leperditia* and the gastropod *Poleumita* cf. *globosa* (Schlotheim). The higher bands, 35 to 57 m above the base of the formation, are rich in bivalves including *Carditomantea*, *Modiolopsis* and *Eurymyella*, with *Leperditia*, eurypterid fragments, the alga *Pachytheca*, and fish including *Pteraspis leathensis*. The siltstones have not been found in the Hereford district.

The characteristic faunal remains are of ostracoderm fish, common but fragmentary in the conglomeratic beds, but less common, though less fragmentary and possibly articulated, in the sandstones (Table 2 and Figure 8). Fragmentary carbonaceous plant remains are common in the channel sandstones, as is *Beaconites antarcticus* (Allen and Williams, 1981b), a large tubular burrow. Cross sections of these burrows, circular to elliptical in shape and 6 to 17 cm in diameter, are common on a bedding surface in the Linton Tile Works [6671 5388], east of Bromyard. Examples up to 20 cm across have been seen at another locality [5568 5872], truncated by a ripple-marked surface.

### Sandstones and conglomerates

These range in thickness from less than 1 m to about 10 m. They rest on scoured erosion surfaces which mark the floors of the original river channels. The bases of many sedimentary cycles are marked by lenticular conglomerate beds 0.1 to 0.5 m thick, and locally cosets reach up to 2 m or more. These beds, usually indurated and forming strong features, are the Type A conglomerates of the main distributary channels of Allen and Williams (1979), and consist of pebbles of calcrete and mudstone in a quartzose sand matrix with a calcareous cement. They are lag deposits formed in the deepest parts of the channels. Individual beds can be massive, or show low-angle planar cross-stratification (see Plate 5), and some contain thin lenses of sandstone and grade into sandstones with scattered clasts of intraformational origin. Several conglomeratic lenses can occur in the lower part of a sandstone sequence, irregularly interbedded with sandstones. Where a conglomerate is absent the lower part of the sandstone may contain sparse pebble-grade clasts of calcrete and mudstone, and cavities are formed where these weather out. Fragmentary water-sorted vertebrate remains are common in the conglomerates, and drifted plant fragments occur in the associated sandstones.

The channel sandstones of the St Maughans Formation are generally finer grained, less conspicuously micaceous, and more pervaded with purple-brown tones than their Raglan Mudstone counterparts. Most are red-brown to purple-brown although some can be yellow-brown, olive-brown or green-grey. Each channel unit shows an overall upward decrease in grain size. The lower parts of the sandstones are typically medium grained and contain abundant parallel-laminated beds formed at a low angle to the general deposition surface, low-angle planar cross-stratification (Plates 4 and 5), and subordinate large-scale trough cross-stratification. The flat-bedded deposits commonly exhibit primary current lineations, observed in situ at a number of localities. Their dominant trend is north-east to south-west on the Bromyard plateau, although the general current

**Plate 5** St Maughans Formation in a small disused quarry [5765 5339], Pencombe.

Low angle planar cross-bedded sandstone and intraformational conglomerate sets are internally parallel and low angle cross-laminated (A14165)

direction in the Hereford area deduced from cross-stratification is towards the south-east (Figure 9). This localised trend may indicate uplift along the Malvern axis with reworked sediments being transported south-westwards into the Bromyard plateau area. The preponderance of parallel laminations implies a persistent unidirectional current with relatively large stream power (Allen, 1964, p.89; 1974b, p.143).

The upper parts of the sandstones are generally finer grained and parallel- to cross-laminated. Ripple-drift bedding and ripple-marked surfaces abound, and a platy to flaggy fissility is imparted by muscovite flakes. The sandstones pass rapidly upwards into micaceous silty mudstones.

Thin sections show the sandstones to be similar to those of the Raglan Mudstone. Garnet is generally much less abundant, however, and there is an increase in the amount of fine-grained igneous and sedimentary rock fragments, notably chert. Heavy mineral analysis of six Hereford sandstones confirms that garnet (mean 70.0 per cent), though still dominant, is less abundant than in the Raglan Mudstone, and that the decrease is compensated for by an increase in apatite (14.5 per cent). Rutile (2.5 per cent), tourmaline (6.5 per cent) and zircon (4.6 per cent) are also more abundant. Epidote, staurolite and chromite are very minor constituents. These results agree with studies in the Clee Hills (Allen, 1974b; Allen and Crowley, 1983), which showed that the main provenence of these sediments was the Lower Palaeozoic volcanic and sedimentary rocks of what is now the Irish Sea and its bordering lands (Figure 6B). However, the most important trend is an upward influx of apatite, a mineral primarily of igneous parentage, and this was not recorded in the earlier studies. Since they are largely derived from pre-existing sediments, the sandstones are generally finer grained, better sorted and more mature than those of the Raglan Mudstone, despite their more proximal source area. In keeping with deposition in a more proximal part of the alluvial plain, Allen (1979, 1983) concluded that the sandstones of the St Maughans Formation were deposited by both braided and meandering streams.

The sandstone and conglomerate beds are normally well jointed and carry a substantial fissure flow of water. The bases of the units are usually marked by strong springs, for example the Cross Well [5136 5138]. The hard water favours tufa formation, and the fissures are commonly lined with travertine in cuttings or excavations [e.g. 5083 5081].

## Mudstones and calcretes

The silty mudstones are similar to those of the Raglan Mudstone though the blocky beds are generally not as thick, and purple-red-brown tones are prominent. They contain, especially near their bases, rapid alternations of fine-grained, micaceous, flaggy sandstones and shaly siltstones in which desiccation cracks are common. A good example is on the sole of a sandstone forming the overhung lip of a waterfall near Grendon Bishop [5910 5788]. Strong sand-filled casts, left after the removal of the underlying mudstone, form polygons up to 0.6 m across (Plate 6). The upper parts of the mudstones are generally calcreted like those of the Raglan Mudstone Formation and profiles of both Types A

**Plate 6**   Dessication crack casts on the sole of a sandstone in the St Maughans Formation.

The sandstone, overlying blocky red-brown siltstone, forms the lip of a small waterfall [5910 5788]. This is a typical situation in the many small gulleys of the Bromyard plateau though erosional channelled bases to the sandstones are more common (A14161)

and B occur (Figure 10). There may be several immature carbonate zones between the major sandstones, and they compose perhaps 50 per cent of the thinner argillaceous beds. In the lowest 30 m of the formation two or three more mature beds can be classified as limestones. They are apparently discontinuous and usually 0.3 to 1 m thick. For example, a limestone 0.3 to 0.4 m thick occurs about 4 m above the Bishop's Frome Limestone, and is exposed several times by a stream in Westfield Wood [5662 5107]. It may be the bed recorded by Clarke (1952b) on Dinmore Hill. Similar mature concretionary limestones probably occur sporadically throughout the formation [e.g. 5843 5359; 5857 5984; 5588 5454; 5912 5909; 601 517]. A mature calcrete, 2 m thick, was exposed during excavations at Durstone Farm [5972 5416], and a similar bed some 20 m higher in the sequence, crops out to the west. Some of these beds may correlate with the following limestone.

The Hackley Limestone Member is a mature concretionary bed of the same type as the Bishop's Frome Limestone Member, and lies approximately 350 to 400 m above it. It contains concretions up to 0.3 m across, and is locally over 5 m thick, forming strong features. It can be traced for several kilometres on the eastern limb of the Bredenbury Anticline, south-west and north-west of Bromyard: the same bed may emerge at Crowels Ash [622 525] on the western limb of the fold. Locally, south-east of Hackley Farm [636 534], the member occurs as two limestones split by several metres of mudstone. There are several disused lime pits near Hackley Farm, and two reveal 0.4 to 0.5 m of the rubbly lower limestone [6396 5296; 6370 5321]. A stream [6332 5336] exposes the basal 0.4 m of limestone on 0.4 m of mudstone. The limestone is probably cut out over parts of the area by channelling by the overlying coarse beds.

# FOUR

# Carboniferous dolerite

A dyke-like intrusion of 'greenstone' at Lowe's (Loose) Hill quarry [5663 4045], near Bartestree (Figure 2), was indicated on Greenough's geological map of 1819, and was first described by Murchison (1834c, p.91; 1839, pp.185–186). By 1839 the rock had long been worked for roadmetal, and the quarry face then extended 37 m compared with 145 m today. Reynolds (1908) gave the first modern petrographical account of the dyke.

The intrusion strikes at 65°, and is 13.5 m wide at the west-south-west end of the quarry [5643 4044]. It has been mapped from surface evidence for 45 m west-south-west of the quarry and for 25 m to the east-north-east i.e. a total length of 215 m. BGS magnetic traverses (Arthur, 1982) indicate that it extends no farther than the mapped limit to the west-south-west, but for 85 m or possibly 215 m to the east-north-east of the quarry. This suggests that the dyke shelves downwards from the east-north-east end of the outcrop before terminating. At the present time, intrusive rock is seen only in the west-south-west end of the quarry, the sides of the quarry being of hornfelsed silty mudstone dipping at 5° to 12° to the west-south-west. Subvertical joints, commonly dipping to the north and roughly parallel with the dyke, also cut the indurated country rock. Calcareous cornstones are readily identifiable even in the most intense zone of metamorphism, and the hornfels superficially resembles an amygdaloidal basalt. The thermal alteration extends for about 4 m outwards on each side of the dyke (Reynolds, 1908, p.502).

Reynolds noted that the intrusion is complex, and 'composed of several allied though differing types of dolerite and basalt'. He suggested that there were three successive injections of basic material: green dolerite without olivine, found chiefly near the southern margin; darker coarser teschenite (olivine-analcime dolerite), which was completely solidified before the latest intrusion; basalt, which forms the central and major portion of the dyke.

Reynolds considered that the dyke was of Carboniferous age, from its petrological similarity to other Midland dolerites of this age. His view has been confirmed by radiometric age determinations of 260 ± 20 million years and 286 ± 18 million years (Fitch and Miller, 1964, pp.163–165; Fitch and others, 1970, p.778). The older date was assumed to relate to the initial consolidation, which was followed by shearing some 30 million years later. These authors also suggested that 286 million years was a minimum age for the consolidation of the magma, and that the dyke may have been intruded about 295 million years ago at a late stage of the Variscan Orogeny, coeval with other bodies of similar composition in the region.

# FIVE

# Structure

## INTRODUCTION

The structure of the Hereford district is relatively simple. The rocks of the Lower Old Red Sandstone have generally low to moderate dips and are cut by a broadly rectangular fault system with the major components trending about north-east–south-west (Caledonoid) and north-west–south-east (Charnoid). Some of the fold axes in the east follow the same trends. Figure 12 outlines the major faults and fold axes.

The district can be divided structurally into two parts, roughly separated by the River Lugg. The western part is largely covered by glacial drift, and the solid rocks contain few stratigraphical markers by which folds and faults might be delineated. Dips measured in exposures are generally less than about 10°, and in the drift-free areas of the Dinmore hills the strata dip eastwards at 1 to 3° over an area of about 20 km².

By contrast the structure over the eastern part of the district is more complex, and dips of 25° or more are common. The strata generally young to the north from the Woolhope Dome to the Bromyard plateau, and most folds also plunge northwards. In the latter area the structural grain is north-west–south-east, with a set of *en-échelon* folds

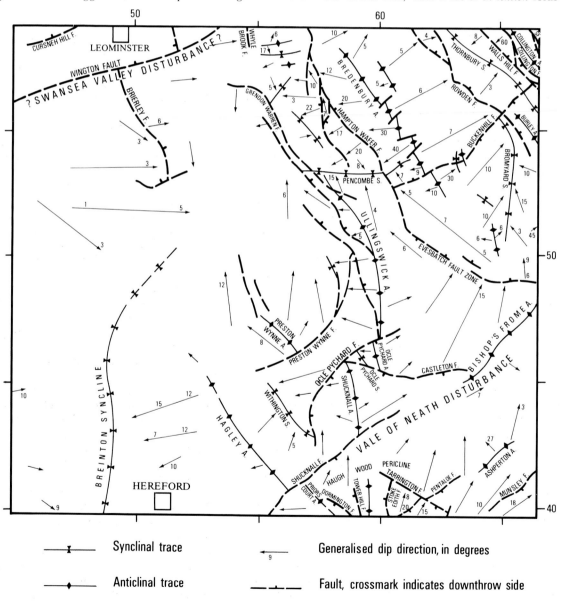

**Figure 12**
Generalised geological structure of the eastern part of the district

| | | |
|---|---|---|
| ——∓—— Synclinal trace | | ←— Generalised dip direction, in degrees |
| ——◆—— Anticlinal trace | | – ∙ – ∙ – Fault, crossmark indicates downthrow side |

F. Fault        S. Syncline        A. Anticline        SF. Steeples Fault subparallel to the trend of the major faulting. The south-west limit of this plexus is marked by the Grendon Warren fault system. A set of minor normal faults trend north-east–south-west. In the south-east most folds, e.g. the Shucknall Hill and Hagley anticlines, trend between north-west–south-east and north–south. Several faults of Caledonoid trend extend into the area from the south-west. The most important of these is the Shucknall Fault, part of the Vale of Neath Disturbance (Owen 1953, 1974). There are several approximately east–west faults in the Much Cowarne [621 472] area and east–west folds such as the Pencombe Syncline and minor folds in the Steen's Bridge area [560 570].

The Lower Old Red Sandstone of the area is considered to have had a low burial depth on the basis of major smectite in the clay minerals of the Townsend Tuff Bed (Merriman, 1988; Parker and others, 1983) and the presence of epidote in the heavy mineral suite of the sandstones. A maximum overburden of 1 km is envisaged, and could well have been considerably less.

## AGE OF TECTONICS

It is now generally accepted (Reading, 1980; Badham, 1982; Owen and Weaver, 1983; Woodcock, 1984a and b) that in much of Wales and the Welsh Borderland the structure of the plastically deformed sedimentary cover is related to fundamental weaknesses in the underlying rigid continental crust. This is particularly true of the several linear structures, for example the Vale of Neath Disturbance, which can be mapped at the surface from south-west to north-east across South Wales and can be related to deep-seated magnetic anomalies. These fractures, commonly with significant strike-slip components, have had long histories of response to the tectonic stresses of successive periods of earth movement. The rocks of the district were deposited in about 25 million years (420–395 million years ago) straddling the Silurian–Devonian boundary (Holland, 1985). The structural disturbances most probably occurred during the climax of the Caledonian Orogeny and during the later Variscan movements, though there is no local supportive stratigraphical control.

Local minor intra-Silurian earth movements in the period leading up to the Caledonian climax are indicated by thinning of the Ludlow sediments towards Gorsley on the Woolhope–May Hill axis (Lawson, 1954; Worssam and others, *in press*), though the conformable passage from marine Silurian to continental molasse in the Welsh Borders shows that local movements were minimal. A period of uplift is marked by a major pedogen at the top of the Raglan Mudstone Formation (Allen, 1985, p.95). There may also have been movement along the Malvern line during deposition of the St Maughans Formation (p.19)

At the culmination of the Caledonian Orogeny, lateral motion along deep-seated north-east–south-west strike-slip faults was very important, taking up the major compressional stresses and initiating folds (Anderton and others, 1979; Reading, 1980; Ziegler, 1982). These zones of strike-slip movement cross Wales and the Welsh Borders as major Caledonoid lineaments, separated by broader, relatively undisturbed belts about 20 km wide. Syndepositional, late Or-dovician to early Devonian, dextral movement took place along these zones, accompanied by dip-slip displacements. The mid-Old Red Sandstone tectonic maximum was presaged by a change to molasse facies in the Lower Old Red Sandstone, and is represented in areas adjacent to the Hereford district (e.g. south of Ross-on-Wye, see Figure 1) by an unconformity along which less-disturbed Upper Old Red Sandstone rests directly on Lower Old Red Sandstone.

In the Hereford district, sinistral movement during the later Variscan Orogeny was probably accommodated along the old Caledonoid lines of weakness, while dextral movement reactivated deep-seated north-west–south-east or north-north-west–south-south-east faults. The orogeny was polyphase (Rast, 1983, p.2) with pulses of deformation in the late Devonian (Bretonic), in middle Carboniferous (Sudetic), and in late Carboniferous (Asturic) times.

## CALEDONOID STRUCTURES

The line of the Vale of Neath Disturbance is picked out by the Dinedor Hill horst (Brandon and Hains, 1979) south of Hereford, and extends into the Hereford district along the valley of the River Frome (Frontispiece). The Shucknall Fault, the major surface expression of the lineament, probably dips steeply to the south-east and throws down more than 200 m in that direction. It is probably the continuation of the Rough Hill Fault on the north side of Dinedor Hill. If post-Ludlovian strike-slip has occurred along the line of the Neath Disturbance in the Hereford district as proposed by Squirrell and Tucker (1960, pp.168–169) it must have been minimal, for not only is there a close match of the Ludlow successions across the Frome valley (Squirrell and Tucker, 1960; Mohamad, 1981, p.33), but there is little evidence for such structural elements as oblique *en-échelon* folds and conjugate shears which are consequent on strike-slip movement (Wilcox and others, 1973; Reading, 1980; Sanderson and Marchini, 1984). The main component of Caledonian movement on the Shucknall Fault was thus probably dip-slip, which was responsible for drag folding and the sharp closure or plunge of the Shucknall Anticline.

The Shucknall Fault has been postulated to extend to Monkhide [608 439], and inconsistent dip readings between Newtown [617 449] and Stretton Grandison [632 440] in the River Lodon and its tributary may indicate its proximity. The broad Bishop's Frome Anticline, plunging to the north-east, lies on the line of the Neath Disturbance, but there is no evidence of any associated faulting. Beyond Bishop's Frome [666 485] the line of the disturbance cannot be traced.

Most of the other Caledonoid structures in the district are speculative. A fault south-east of Tarrington is probably continuous with the Pentaloe Fault, which Squirrell and Tucker (1960, pl.25) traced across the Woolhope upfold to Mordiford. Unlike the adjacent Rock Fault and other Caledonoid faults in the Woolhope area, along which dextral strike-slip as well as dip-slip movement have been postulated, the Pentaloe Fault was assumed by them to be of normal type, throwing down 9 to 30 m to the south-east. It is possibly displaced by a later north-west–south-east fault at Tarrington, beyond which the throw diminishes rapidly. The Ashperton Anticline, on the line of the Pentaloe Fault, has limbs dipping at about 10° to 15°, though higher dips are recorded on the north-west side.

Possible strike-slip movement along the Ocle Pychard and Preston Wynne faults is suggested by their truncation and presumed dextral displacement of fold axes.

The Ivington Fault is marked by a zone of disturbed strata south-east of Eaton [512 580] across which there is apparently very little vertical displacement. The nearby Cursneh Hill Fault has a downthrow to the north of 130 m. These faults mark the line of the Swansea Valley Disturbance or a southerly splay from it. This disturbance probably runs through the drift-covered ground from Dilwyn [416 545] to Weobley [403 515] and coincides with the northern margin of gravity and magnetic anomalies of Caledonoid trend beneath which the basement rocks are possibly at relatively shallow depth (p.25).

## CHARNOID STRUCTURES

The structures of the Bromyard plateau have been interpreted as the results of plastic deformation of the upper crustal layer of Lower Palaeozoic rocks above planes of brittle fracture shear in the Precambrian basement, mainly during the post-Westphalian phase of the Variscan Orogeny. Phipps and Reeve (1969, p.31) also proposed such an origin for the Ledbury and Colwall faults nearer the Malvern line. These authors discounted simple regional east–west horizontal compression, and suggested that the basement was the controlling factor in the regional tectonics. The shears probably mark zones of weakness in the basement very much older than either the Caledonian or Variscan episodes. Near the surface the major north-west–south-east faults are probably almost vertical with steep dips to the north-east; they may be reverse fractures overthrust to the west, such as the Collington Fault, or normal faults (p.25). The Collington Fault is probably an extension of the Colwall Fault in the Malverns.

The Collington Anticline to the east has the same oblique en-échelon relationship to the Collington Fault as the Mathon folds have to the Colwall Fault and the Ledbury folds to the Ledbury Fault (Phipps and Reeve, 1969, pp.24, 26), implying analagous sinistral displacement. The Colwall Fault has been interpreted as a major, near-vertical, sinistral fault, with a large vertical component and a lateral displacement of about 1200 m at Colwall, decreasing to 300 m towards the south-east. The lateral displacement along the Collington Fault may be comparable in magnitude, and here the vertical component is about 100 m. It is probable that the adjacent and parallel Wall Hills Fault, with a normal throw of several hundreds of metres, may have been a partner wrench, with the dip of the beds between the two faults increasing to 70° and even to the vertical. The change in attitude of the Burley Anticline and the Bromyard Syncline may also be associated with sinistral dispacement along these faults.

South-west of the Collington structures the similar Pencombe [600 528] plexus between the Bredenbury and Ullingswick anticlines may be associated with sinistral movement along the Grendon Warren Fault or one of the several parallel fractures. This fault may be continuous with the Whyle Brook Fault [546 590], and to the south-east may run into the Evesbatch Fault Zone.

Away from the Bromyard plateau there are relatively few north-west–south-east faults, and none that can be associated with strike-slip movement. South of Leominster the Brierley Fault throws 70 m down to the east. Near Preston Wynne [558 471] it is possible that two faults obliquely truncate the poorly defined Preston Wynne Anticline. The Hagley Anticline is complementary to the Withington Syncline and forms the flattened dome of the Ludlow inlier of Hagley Park [561 409]. The ground is poorly exposed but the few dips recorded appear to confirm its presence as far as the Lugg Valley. To the south-east it may continue as the Priors Court Anticline, offset sinistrally by the Shucknall Fault.

The Shucknall Anticline, trending nearly north–south, is a relatively tight asymmetrical fold. In Shucknall quarry [5915 4306] (see Plate 1) the eastern limb dips at 35 to 47° and possibly up to 70°, and the western limb at about 17°. Northwards in the Shucknall inlier the axial plane of the fold coincides in places with a fault throwing down to the west; the steep eastern limb persists and the fold can be traced in the Raglan Mudstone, plunging northwards, as far as the Ocle Pychard and Castleton faults. Southwards the Shucknall Anticline closes sharply against the Shucknall Fault, on the northern side of which steep southerly dips are recorded.

The composite Woolhope Anticline, trending north-west–south-east, has a steeper western limb (Squirrell and Tucker, 1960). In the northern part of the inlier, the main axis of the upfold is complicated by two subsidiary anticlinal flexures, the Priors Court Anticline and the Haugh Wood Pericline. Sparse outcrops in the Raglan Mudstone Formation between Dormington and Bartestree suggest that the former fold continues to the east of the Bartestree dyke as far as the Shucknall Fault. The Haugh Wood Pericline trends about north–south and plunges to the north at about 15°, presumably dying out north of Perton. The northern end of the pericline is cut by several minor faults trending about north–south. The Stoke Edith Fault is the largest with a westerly downthrow of about 70 m. Squirrell and Tucker (1960, p.164) remarked that the throws of many of these fractures decrease to the north, dying out as the amplitude of the fold decreases. They are presumably normal faults formed by the doming. Theories of the formation of the main north-west–south-east fold pattern of Woolhope and Shucknall have been discussed by Squirrell and Tucker (1960, p.179).

## ARMORICANOID STRUCTURES

In the Newtown-Much Cowarne area [615 465] the Castleton Fault truncates and possibly offsets the Ocle Pychard folds in a dextral sense. The Pencombe Syncline, the largest of several folds on the west side of the Bromyard plateau, cuts across the predominantly north-west–south-east grain and forms the closure of the Ullingswick Anticline.

## SEISMICITY

The Hereford region is one of the most seismically active parts of Britain (Lilwall, 1976). A zone of higher than average seismic activity follows a Caledonoid trend from South Wales into the Midlands, with Hereford apparently in the area of maximum intensity. The tremors are characteristically deep events (30–60 km) for continental crust (Jackson and Muir Wood, 1980, p.717), and are thus felt over large areas but with relatively low maximum intensities. Many minor quakes (some 23 in 200 years) were documented by Davison (1924, pp.244–259), with strong events on 6 October 1863 (maximum intensity 8 on Davison's Scale), 30 October 1868 (7 DS) and 17 December 1896 (8 DS). No less than eleven shocks occurred on this last date, and damage was caused to chimneys and to part of the Cathedral. Another notable quake (maximum intensity 7 DS) occurred on 15 August 1926 (Oldham, 1926; Davison, 1927; Jeffreys, 1927). Though Davison (1924, p.257; 1927, p.166) believed that the earthquakes were centred on local twin foci, recent reappraisals of historical records by BGS (Musson and others, 1984) show that the more important events were more scattered with separate epicentres outside the present district. Only three relatively shallow, minor earthquakes with epicentres in the Hereford district have been recorded by the more accurate BGS seismograph network since 1979, and discussion of the causative structures is considered premature. A magnitude 0.7 shock occurred at an undetermined depth beneath Hope under Dinmore [350 253] on 14 May 1980, a magnitude 0.1 tremor occurred at 11.3 km depth beneath Wellington [485 479] on 20 May 1983, and a magnitude 0.3 event occurred at 5.9 km depth beneath Marden [534 473] on 20 August 1984.

## GEOPHYSICAL SURVEYS

The margins of the geological map carry extracts at a scale of 1:250 000 from the BGS gravity anomaly and aeromagnetic anomaly maps of Britain.

The gravity anomalies do not reflect the distribution of the rocks at the surface, but are generally attributable to relief on the upper surface of the deep Precambrian basement. Because the basement rocks are commonly denser than those nearer the surface, a gravity high can result from an area of shallower basement, and vice versa. The Palaeozoic rocks may be separated from the basement by a surface of decollement formed during one or more of the orogenic episodes that have affected the district. The aeromagnetic anomalies are also unrelated to the surface rocks, and reflect the distribution of relatively more magnetic rocks within the basement.

The aeromagnetic and gravity fields are broadly comparable. A broad gravity low in the south-east coincides with a generally low aeromagnetic field. The deepest part of this aeromagnetic low has a Caledonoid trend and is probably bounded to the north-west by the Vale of Neath Disturbance. Similarly in the west between Norton Canon [380 475] and Aulden [462 548], an aeromagnetic high trends north-east–south-west and coincides with a gravity high. Quantitative interpretation of the aeromagnetic high indicates that at its centre [c.400 475] the basement may rise to within about 400 m of ground level from a general depth of about 2000 m (Arthur, 1982, fig. E.8). The north-western margin of these coincident highs may correspond with the position of the Swansea Valley Disturbance in the basement (p.24).

The Collington Borehole [646 610], to the north of Bromyard (p.13), started in the Raglan Mudstone and cut presumed Precambrian basement at about 1700 m below ground level. In 1984 BGS commissioned a seismic reflection line, linked to an earlier confidential seismic survey and to the borehole. The results of this survey (Chadwick, 1985a, fig. 1.3; 1985b) indicate a fairly level upper surface to the basement at about 1800 m depth, which agrees with the borehole results and the regional geophysical data. The seismic line shows that major steep north-west–south-east faults develop upwards from low-angle listric faults which dip north-eastwards at 20 to 30° in the basement, and on which reactivated reverse movement has taken place. The north-west–south-east faults of the Bromyard plateau are probably analogous structures (p.24).

# SIX

# Quaternary

## INTRODUCTION

The glacial deposits of England and Wales have long been divided into Older and Newer Drift (Jukes-Browne, 1887; Charlesworth, 1929). This concept is still usefully applied in the Hereford District although the Quaternary Deposits as a whole can be divided into four groups (see geological succes-

sion inside front cover). The oldest group, the Older Drift, mostly occurs east of the River Lugg as small relict areas of till and outwash gravel from a pre-Devensian glaciation. The second oldest group consists of remnants of a flight of four gravel terraces of the River Lugg. The third group, the Newer Drift, is the product of the last glaciation; this left extensive deposits west of the Lugg, largely obliterating the

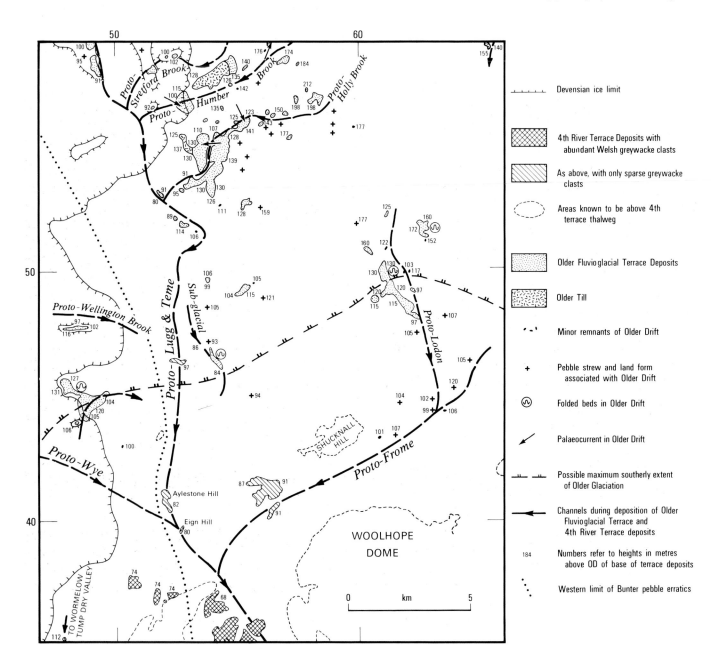

**Figure 13**  Distribution of remnants of Older Drift and Fourth River Terrace Deposits

evidence of the earlier glaciation. This glaciation was of Late Devensian age, lasting from about 26 000 to 14 000 years ago. Its deposits include tills, gravels of various types and substantial deposits of head formed beyond the ice-margin. The youngest group of Quaternary sediments, including river alluvium, colluvium and peat, belongs to the post-glacial Flandrian stage, dating from about 10 000 years ago to the present.

## OLDER DRIFT DEPOSITS

The oldest deposits, formerly more widespread, include patches of till and irregular fluvioglacial[1] gravel terraces thought to be the deposits of a single pre-Devensian glacia-

1 The term fluvioglacial has been used throughout the memoir although glaciofluvial is now considered the more correct term.

tion. They form hill cappings or patches on benches or spurs, and were deposited when the local base level was 35 to 45 m higher than at present and the general relief less dissected. Their distribution is shown in Figure 13.

### Older Till

Thin patches of till occur on higher ground outside the Devensian ice-limit south-east of Leominster, where temporary exposures north of Steen's Bridge [540 575] showed up to 2 m of red-brown, finely sandy, stony silt, with clasts, some of which are ice-striated, ranging from granules to cobbles. The presence locally of a thin bed of stoneless sand and the silty, earthy nature of the deposit are indicative of melt-out ablation till rather than a lodgement deposit. A resistivity traverse suggests that beds of till are also probably present within the northern part of the large sand and gravel remnant near Risbury Bridge. About 1.3 m of red-brown,

**Plate 7**  Older fluvioglacial gravels in the Upper Lyde Pit [4925 4472], Burghill–Portway (see Figure 14).

Well-stratified gravels of variable coarseness and sorting, consist almost entirely of Old Red Sandstone clasts; the large pebbles and cobbles are of sandstone and the smaller pebbles of calcrete nodules. Imbrication in the coarser beds indicates a current direction to the north-east (left to right) (A13287)

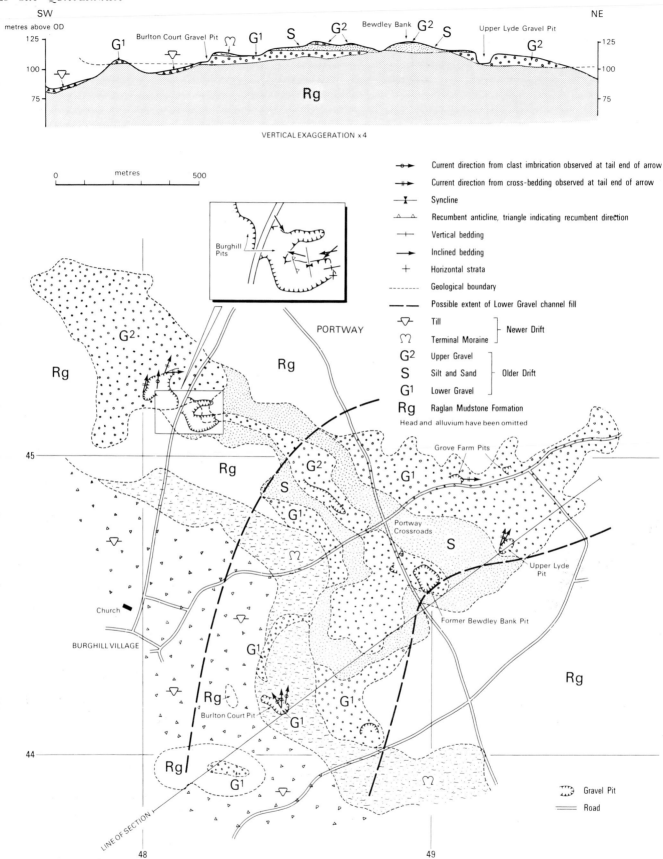

**Figure 14** Older Fluvioglacial Terrace Deposits and the maximum extent of the Newer Drift in the Burghill–Portway area

**Figure 15**  Rock-head contours showing the channel form beneath the Older Fluvioglacial Terrace Deposits on Sutton Hill

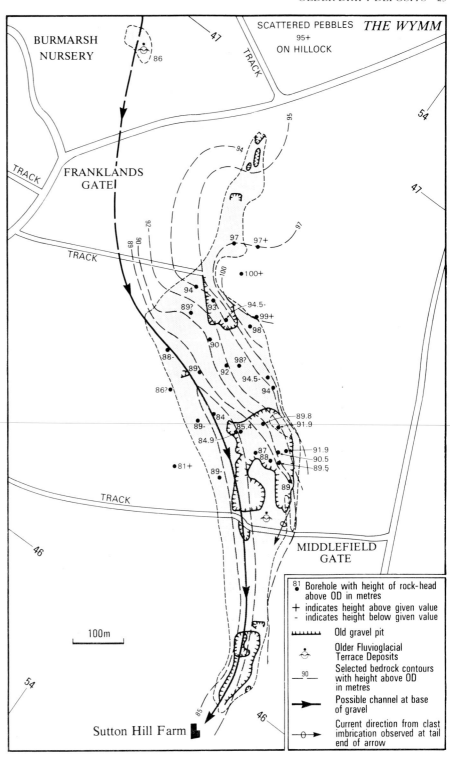

## Older Fluvioglacial Terrace Deposits

stiff, stony, clayey silt exposed in the bed of a stream at Low Brook [5434 5488] is possibly a lodgement till. The lowest 4 m of beds at Windmill Hill [6063 4870], consisting of unstructured, coarse gravel with a high proportion of sandy silt, may be ablation till. They are overlain by finer washed gravel. Till has also been seen in a now infilled pit nearby at Stoke Hill [613 496] (Hodgson, 1972, p.14).

These deposits consist mostly of gravel, with subordinate beds ranging from clay and silt to coarse, granular sand. They are thought to have been washed from the pre-Devensian ice during its advance and retreat, and to have completely filled minor channels and formed spreads along the broader valleys. Some deposits show evidence of standing ice in close proximity, and some may include washed periglacial deposits.

The deposits are of very variable thickness, locally up to 20 m. Many have been worked and during the survey good sections were open at Pudleston [5637 5903], Blackwardine [e.g. 5267 5672], Risbury [5395 5495], Uphampton Farm [5714 5827], Court Hill [5220 5572 and 5547 5598], Burghill–Portway [e.g. 4925 4472 (Plate 7)], Sutton Hill [541 464], Norton Court [5379 4957], Windmill Hill [6065 4872], Stoke Hill [6224 4872] and Crick's Green [6270 5160 and 6273 5125]. The gravels are characteristically immature, being generally poorly sorted and poorly stratified, with a wide range of mainly subangular pebble sizes and a high fines content of red-brown clay to sand. They contain lenses and beds of better sorted fine gravel and pebbly sand. Coarse cobble and boulder gravels intergrade with ablation till at some localities, such as Burghill–Portway, Norton Court, Sutton Hill, Windmill Hill and Bowley Town [5405 5310] (Dwerryhouse and Miller, 1930, p.113). Typically the fluvioglacial gravels contain more clasts of the less durable local Old Red Sandstone calcretes and sandstones than do the more mature fluvial gravels of the later river terraces, though the most durable and farthest travelled erratics, such as Welsh greywacke and Bunter pebbles, are conspicuous in the ploughland due to the progressive removal of the local clasts by carbonate leaching and weathering.

The Older Drift deposits are generally more weathered, indurated and cryoturbated than their Devensian counterparts, and have also undergone more extensive leaching and redistribution of carbonate. The older gravels contain irregular, cemented lenses of secondary lime enrichment up to about 2 m thick and 5 m wide; solution fissures with white encrustations of lime, not seen in the Devensian deposits, are also common.

The bases of the deposits generally overlie uneven surfaces; gravels are commonly banked steeply against bedrock. Many of the remnants probably fill ancient valleys, and some were possibly subglacial (Figure 13). For example the lower gravel at Burghill–Portway, deposited by a current flowing towards the north and north-east, is restricted to a 12 m deep, 700 m wide channel cut into bedrock (Figure 14 and Plate 7). A further example, the Sutton Hill deposit, is probably a channel-fill with most of the south-west flank eroded away (Figure 15). Pebble imbrication indicates flow to the south-south-east. The base level of 84 m above OD is lower than the possible base level of the slightly younger Fourth River Terrace at 97 m above OD on Sutton Walls (Figure 18), suggesting that the Sutton Hill channel was subglacial. Slumped and contorted beds at this locality confirm the former presence of ice. Deposits at Adzor Bank [480 477] are probably infill remnants of the southern flank of a proto-Wellington Brook valley.

South-east of Leominster gravel deposits are the remains of the infillings of the Older Drift channels of the proto-Humber, proto-Holly and proto-Stretford brooks (Figures 16, 17 and 21A and B). Palaeocurrent directions, deduced from pebble imbrication and cross-bedding, indicate that deposition was obliquely across the old valleys to the south-east at Court Hill and Blackwardine and up the proto-Humber Brook to the north-north-east at Pudleston (Figure 17). These directions indicate a prograding delta preceding the advancing ice sheet from the west or north-west.

Within the gorge of the Dinmore Hill meander at Hampton Court Bridge [519 529] and The Rookery [526 518] the Older Drift gravels are banked steeply against solid rock on both sides. They occur as low as 80 m above OD, suggesting

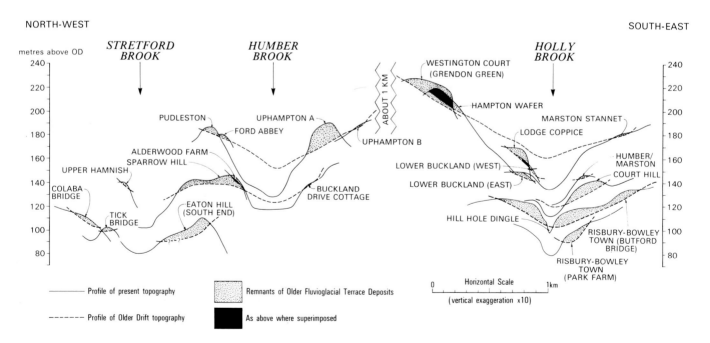

**Figure 16**  Profiles of the Older Fluvioglacial Terrace remnants along the valleys of Humber, Holly and Stretford brooks. The terrace bases generally dip towards the present brook at about the same gradient. Figure 17 shows their locations. For each valley the remnants are seen to drop in height progressively in a downstream direction

**Figure 17** Old Drift remnants of the Proto-Humber, Proto-Holly and Proto-Stretford brooks

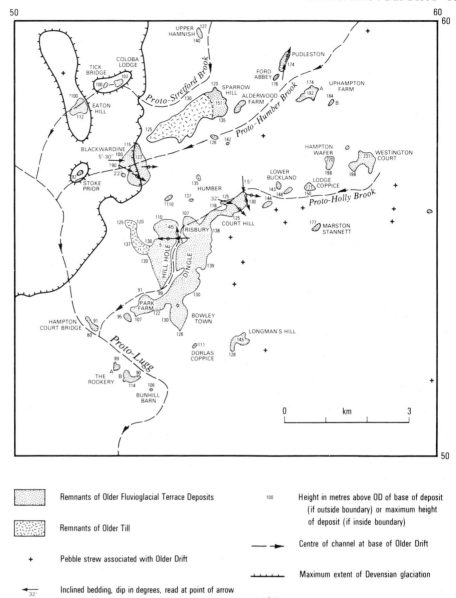

Remnants of Older Fluvioglacial Terrace Deposits

Remnants of Older Till

+ Pebble strew associated with Older Drift

Inclined bedding, dip in degrees, read at point of arrow

Current direction deduced from clast imbrication or cross-bedding, read at tail of arrow

100 Height in metres above OD of base of deposit (if outside boundary) or maximum height of deposit (if inside boundary)

Centre of channel at base of Older Drift

Maximum extent of Devensian glaciation

Devensian nunatak

that a subglacial channel, probably of the proto-Lugg/Teme system, existed on the north side of the Dinmore Hill spur in pre-Devensian times and that the incised meander has existed for a considerable period.

Beds probably deposited close to wasting masses of stagnant ice are found at three localities (Figure 13). Those at Crossways [613 496], on Stoke Hill, are no longer exposed, but steep eastward dips, commonly up to 60° and in places even vertical, have been recorded in bouldery gravels and thick silts (Luckman, 1970, p.189; Hodgson, 1972, p.14). Similar slump-induced deformation caused by melting of buried ice affect an upper gravel and a median division of sands and silts in the Burghill sand pit [4810 4515] (Figure 14) and illsorted gravels in a pit on Sutton Hill [541 464] (Figure 15). Recumbent folds and vertical bedding occur with no overall trend, and small-scale normal faults are seen at Sutton Hill.

A line from Stoke Hill to Burghill may mark the max-

imum southward extent of the pre-Devensian ice sheet (Figure 13). South of it there is no direct evidence of former ice. The absence of Older Drift on the high ground of Shucknall Hill [590 430] and Hansnett Wood [660 425], together with the apparent absence of all but 'local drift' (or head) on the Woolhope Dome (Murchison, 1839; Merewether, 1871, pp.173–174; 1887a, pp.18–21) probably indicates that these areas remained unglaciated. Eastwards the ice margin must have swung southwards, as an extensive deposit of Older Till containing abundant Bunter pebbles has recently been discovered in the Coddington area [730 430], on the west side of the Malverns (Brandon, 1988).

A gravel pit at Burlton Court [4847 4416] (Figure 14) shows the Older and Newer Drifts in juxtaposition. Up to 2.3 m of gravelly till of the Devensian terminal moraine, with abundant Lower Palaeozoic sandstones, rest on 10 m of older gravel containing less than 1 per cent of these sandstones. The lower gravels are cryoturbated below the junc-

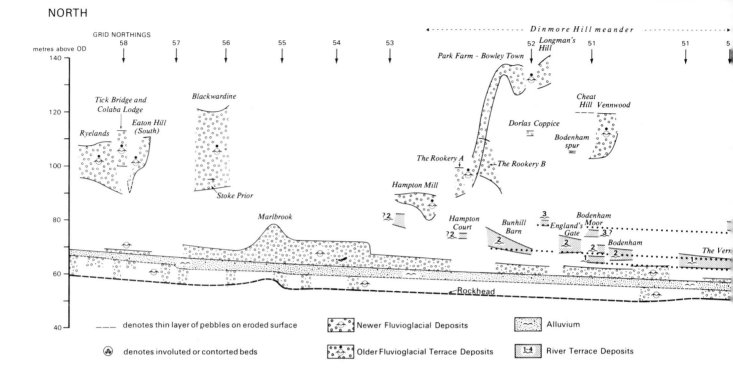

**Figure 18** Longitudinal profiles of the gravel terraces of the Lugg (projected to the centre of the Lugg channel). The total height range of each deposit is shown rather than its thickness at any point. Remnants of Older Fluvioglacial Terrace Deposits are included only if they are close to the River Lugg

tion, with frost-fractured pebbles, some of which have been reoriented vertically. At Blackwardine railway cutting [5310 5661], recently infilled, the deposits of the two glaciations are also adjacent, and here the Devensian glacier probably terminated against an old gravel ridge. A thin cryoturbated stony silt, with numerous Welsh greywacke pebbles, washed from the Devensian ice-margin, overlies 9 m of partially cryoturbated deltaic gravels of the Older Drift. Small faults affect the old gravels in a nearby pit [5278 5645], and may have been formed as the Devensian glacier pushed against the frozen mass of Older Drift.

**Provenance of erratics**

The Older Drift remnants of the district fall into two categories distinguished by different clasts (Figure 13). Those in the north-east contain 55 to 75 per cent subangular to subrounded local Old Red Sandstone material, of which calcrete nodules account for about two thirds and sandstone for most of the rest. There are minor amounts of silty mudstone, cornstone conglomerate and tuffaceous mudstone. The farther-travelled erratics, comprising 25 to 45 per cent of the clasts, suggest a north-western to northern provenance. Abundant Ludlovian sandstones, along with various fossiliferous calcareous siltstones and limestones of Silurian age, have probably been derived from the high ground of the Radnor and Clun Forests and from Aymestrey outcrops to the north-west (Grindley, 1918, p.229). Sporadic

erratics of Hanter's Hill Gabbro (Dwerryhouse and Miller, 1930, p.113 and pl. XII), originating some 32 km north-west of Hereford, indicate ice movement from the west-north-west. A minor component, indicating a west-north-west or north-west provenance in central Wales, consists of quartz-veined Llandovery greywackes and a variety of volcanic rocks. Coal fragments, common in sand lenses at Pudleston and Court Hill, are probably derived from Titterstone Clee Hill 16 km to the north, or the Wyre Forest Coalfield a similar distance to the north-east. The common hard, well rounded clasts of liver-coloured quartzite and red-stained vein-quartz (henceforth called Bunter pebbles) have been derived from the Triassic Kidderminster Conglomerate Formation, and suggest transport from Cheshire, Shropshire or Worcestershire. Rare rounded yellow-brown patinated flints occur at Vennwood [5490 4898] and an Upper Liassic ammonite, probably derived from the Older Drift, is recorded from the 4th Terrace gravels at Lugwardine–Bartestree [560 416] (Richardson, 1911, p.66). These varying directions of provenance suggest that the ice incorporated deposits of an even earlier glaciation, and that the subordinate Mesozoic pebbles of the Hereford area may be secondarily derived. However, probably coeval beds of sand and gravel in the Mathon area [c.735 450] on the west side of the Malvern Hills contain abundant Bunter pebbles, common Liassic *Gryphaea* and coal fragments (Grindley, 1925; Hey, 1959) that were derived from the north-east.

The second category occurs at Adzor Bank and at

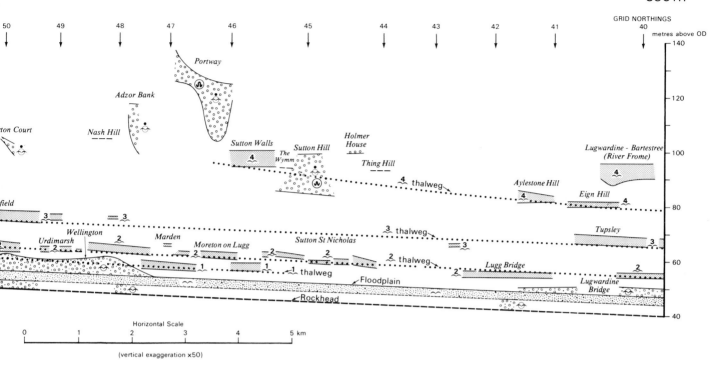

Horizontal Scale

(vertical exaggeration x50)

Burghill – Portway (see also p.38), with extensive remnants 6 to 10 km south-west of Hereford at Kivernoll and Much Dewchurch (Luckman, 1960, p.190), of which Blakemore Hill and Willock's Bridge (Brandon and Hains, 1981, p.19) are the most northern. The clasts consist almost entirely of local Old Red Sandstone (99 per cent in the 4 – 8 mm fraction), with very few Ludlow sandstones and Welsh greywackes. Large blocks of siliceous tuffaceous mudstone from the Raglan Mudstone are very common, but no Bunter pebbles have been found. These gravels may be the outwash from a local ice-sheet emanating from the Black Mountains.

### Age of the Older Drift

The greater weathering and dissection of the deposits, their relatively high base level, and their relationship with the Devensian deposits make it clear that they are older than the deposits ascribed to the Late Devensian glaciation. This was the view of Luckman (1970, pp.187 – 190, fig. 8.3) who first recognised that these deposits dated from an earlier glaciation analogous to the Older Drifts of the Midlands and the lower Severn valley (Wills, 1950). Bowen (1973, fig. 1) was in broad agreement with Luckman's views. Other workers, however, (Dwerryhouse and Miller, 1930, pp.112 – 113; Pocock, 1940, p.102; Hodgson, 1972, pp.13 – 15; Cross and Hodgson, 1975, p.318, fig. 2), have claimed that all the gravel remnants of the district belong to a single Devensian 'Wye Glacier'.

It is thought that only periglacial conditions resulted from the generally cold climates of the Early and Middle Devensian (e.g. Catt, 1981, p.11), and in view of the present uncertain status and possible former limited extent of the penultimate 'Wolstonian' glaciation (Shotton, 1986; Bowen and others, 1986; Rose, 1987), it is believed that the Hereford deposits are more likely to belong to the even earlier Anglian glaciation.

### OLDER RIVER TERRACES

South of Bodenham [530 510] and outside the Devensian ice-limit, the Lugg valley contains the remains of four gravel terraces (Figure 18). Each terrace remnant rests on bedrock and is part of a formerly widespread aggraded sheet. The individual remnants are well separated vertically, with bedrock outcrops between the terrace flats. Details of the terraces are given in Table 3. The high thalweg gradient of the 4th Terrace could suggest that more than one period of aggradation has been included in the deposits of this terrace.

In general the higher the terrace the more it is dissected and the more widely distributed are the remnants. The 1st Terrace is less well preserved than the 2nd, probably because it lies within a few metres of the present flood-plain, and was either largely removed by torrential meltwater during the last glaciation or obscured by outwash gravels. There is some evidence to indicate that prior to the last glaciation the River Lugg was joined by the Teme at Aymestrey and by the Onny at Leominster (Pocock, 1925, p.29; Dwerryhouse and Miller, 1930, p.116) so that the terraces were laid down by a river much larger than the present Lugg and possibly the major river of the area, joined by a tributary proto-Wye at Hereford (Figure 13).

In contrast to the immature outwash gravels of either glaciation, the Lugg terrace fluvial gravels are clean and well

**Table 3**
Details of the Lugg terrace deposits

| Maximum thickness | Height of base above floodplain and OD level at: | | Number | Name | Thalweg gradient (m/km). The floodplain is 0.85 | Possible age |
|---|---|---|---|---|---|---|
| | Hereford | Bodenham | | | | |
| 2 m | 4 m (57 m OD) at Moreton on Lugg | 5 m (66 m OD) | 1st | Marden | 0.92 | Late Devensian |
| 6 m | 7 m (54 m OD) | 8 m (69 m OD) | 2nd | Moreton on Lugg | 0.92 | Late Devensian(?) to Hoxnian(?) |
| 3 m | 18 m (65 m OD) | 19 m (79 m OD) | 3rd | Kingsfield | 0.88 | |
| 7.6 m | 30 m (77 m OD) | 42 m (95 m OD) at Sutton Walls | 4th | Sutton Walls | 2.3(?) | Hoxnian(?) or Late Anglian(?) |

sorted with a relatively sparse sandy matrix. They are well stratified in thin beds and contain lenses of coarse sand up to about 0.5 m thick. Characteristically the beds are cross-bedded, and the tabular clasts are imbricate; variable palaeocurrent directions at any one site suggest deposition from a river meandering across a wide flood plain. The clasts are mainly far-travelled, and comprise mostly fine sandstones of probable Ludlow age, and Silurian limestones, with minor amounts of greywacke from Wales, vein quartz, volcanic rocks, Bunter pebbles, and sporadic examples of Hanter's Hill Gabbro. The main constituents could have been derived from the headwaters of the Lugg/Teme in the Radnor and Clun Forests, but the farther travelled minor constitents are almost certainly derived from the Older Drift.

To the west of Hereford the Devensian glaciation has destroyed any preglacial terraces that may have existed, but to the south-east, outside the district, terraces in the Wye valley are considered to be contemporaneous with those along the Lugg (Brandon and Hains, 1981). These remnants contain far more Llandovery greywacke pebbles from the proto-Wye catchment in central Wales, than the Lugg terrace gravels (Figure 13). The contrast is most clearly demonstrated by a comparison of the components of two adjacent remnants of the 4th Terrace at Hereford. The northern outlier at Aylestone Hill [520 410] has extremely few greywacke clasts and was clearly situated north of the confluence of the Wye and Lugg; on Eign Hill, only 1 km to the south-south-east, the gravel contains roughly 35 per cent of this lithology, and must have been deposited by the proto-Wye.

The river terraces discussed above are tentatively correlated with the four lower down the Wye in the incised meanders of the Monmouth to Chepstow reach (Welch and Trotter, 1961, p.134). However, only a very discontinuous strip of two terraces has been recognised in the intermediate stretch between Holme Lacy and Walford (Whitefield, 1971, fig. 2, p.3; Hodgson and Palmer, 1971, fig. 4, pp.10–11) and a flight of terraces is not recognised at Ross-on-Wye (Smith, 1980).

Like the Older Drift, the surface layers of the river terrace gravels suffered periglaciation during the Devensian period.

Lime redistribution has also taken place in the Sutton Walls Terrace gravels, though to a lesser extent than in the Older Drift.

Although the relative age of the terraces is clear there is little evidence of their absolute ages. Their relationship to the glacial gravels suggests that they are intermediate in age between Older and Newer Drifts though it cannot be entirely discounted that the 4th Terrace in part pre-dates the Older Drift. The 4th Terrace was probably deposited fairly soon after the withdrawal of the pre-Devensian ice. Symonds (1872, pp.165–166) and Dawkins (1869, p.197) recorded finds of the teeth of woolly rhinoceros (*Coelodonta antiquitatis*) and fossil horse (*Equus fossilis* and *E. caballus*, both probably closely related to the modern horse *E. ferus*) from workings in the 4th Terrace at Lugwardine–Bartestree [560 416]. If these fossils are not secondarily derived from the Older Drift, they indicate tundra conditions bordering on steppe (West, 1968, pp.340, 342; Sutcliffe, 1985, table 8) and would support a late-Anglian rather than a Hoxnian age. The 1st Terrace of the Lugg/Teme contains more greywacke clasts than would be expected from reworking of the Older Drift alone, and it may represent the distal outwash from the late-Devensian ice-advance when the ice had carried abundant greywacke debris into the headwaters of the Lugg or Teme.

## NEWER DRIFT DEPOSITS

### Introduction

Towards the end of the Devensian cold stage, about 26 000 years ago, a thick sheet of piedmont ice, formed by the coalescing of several valley glaciers from the accumulating snowfields of central Wales, spread eastwards across the Herefordshire lowlands. The ice advanced to a generally north–south line just west of the River Lugg, except near Leominster where it thrust a short distance across the valley (Figure 19). At its maximum the ice was over 230 m thick in the valleys, for it overran some of the high hills of the district such as Garnons Hill [400 445] (233 m above OD) (Charlesworth, 1929, p.348) and Burton–Wormsley Hill

**Figure 19**
Maximum extent of the Devensian glaciation in Herefordshire as proposed by the major contributors to the Drift geology of the region. The area of the Hereford Sheet (198) is outlined

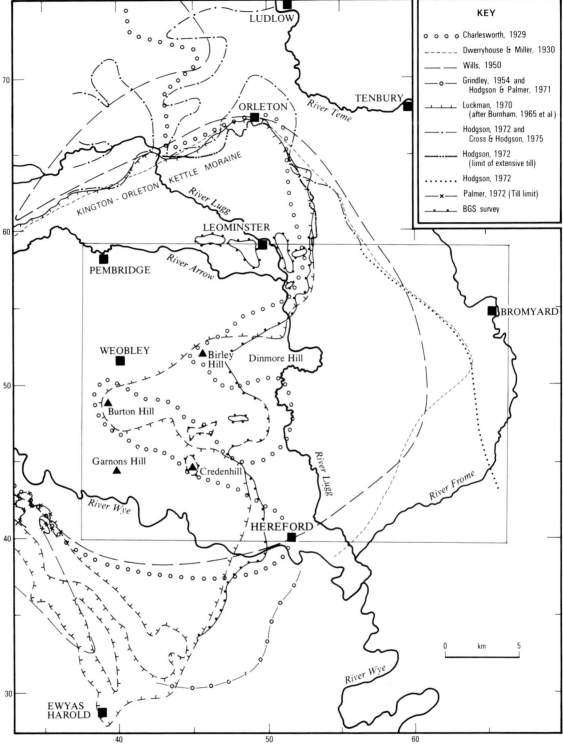

KEY

∘ ∘ ∘ ∘ Charlesworth, 1929
– – – – Dwerryhouse & Miller, 1930
— — — Wills, 1950
—∘—∘— Grindley, 1954 and
          Hodgson & Palmer, 1971
—+—+— Luckman, 1970
          (after Burnham, 1965 et al)
—·—·— Hodgson, 1972 and
          Cross & Hodgson, 1975
—··—··— Hodgson, 1972
          (limit of extensive till)
∙∙∙∙∙∙∙ Hodgson, 1972
—×—×— Palmer, 1972 (Till limit)
▲▲▲▲ BGS survey

[396 488] (294 m above OD). To the south-east Merbach ridge [304 447] was glaciated up to at least 294 m above OD though its summit at 318 m above OD remained ice-free (Grindley, 1911, p.164; Palmer, 1972, p.8). The ice thinned considerably towards its margins, and the tops of Credenhill [450 445] (219 m above OD) and Adzor Bank [479 477] (118 m above OD) remained permanently above the ice as nunataks.

The Newer Drift deposited by the Devensian glaciation has remained largely unchanged since the glacial retreat. It mantles valley floors, hillslopes and interfluves alike, and largely retains its constructional glacial and fluvioglacial geomorphology. It consists of a thin blanket of lodgement and ablation till over much of the area, with a moundy, kamiform complex of till, gravel and silt, characterised by kettle-holes, filling some valleys, notably that of the River Wye. The eastward limit of the ice is marked in places by a narrow linear terminal moraine composed of heterogeneous deposits. Situated well inside the ice margin, some sub-parallel morainic belts (e.g. the Staunton Moraine) may represent successive retreat stages of still-stand or oscillations in the ice retreat. The final glacial deposits were sheet-like fluvioglacial terrace sandar spreads of gravel, silt and sand, mostly connected with the final ablation stage as the climate ameliorated. These spreads built up over much of the low ground within the glacially affected areas and formed extensive areas of outwash immediately beyond the ice-margin, that now form terraces along the Lugg and Wye valleys. The valleys to the east of the Lugg, and east of the ice-sheet, are floored by contemporaneous fluvioperiglacial gravels of local origin derived from soliflucted bedrock and Older Drift material.

The first mention of westerly derived drift of coarse Welsh and local detritus covering the district was by Murchison (1834d, pp.194; 1835, p.231; 1839, pp.510–516) who roughly defined its eastward limit and distinguished it from the northern drift of Shropshire. Subsequently several local workers, including Symonds and Curley in the last century and Aldis, Moore and Grindley in the early years of the present century, have studied the distribution and nature of the glacial deposits in this general area; their results have been published mainly in the Transactions of the Woolhope Naturalists' Field Club. The most recent observations are by Luckman (1970) and Palmer (1972).

It is not possible here to review fully the reasons why various authors have placed the position of the ice-margin in several slightly different positions across the district. Figure 19, however, outlines these postulated positions, and refers to the authors concerned. The terminal ice-front suggested by the recent survey agrees broadly with the limit proposed for the Newer Drift by Charlesworth (1929, p.348 and pl. XXI). Other authors place it much farther to the east near Bromyard on the basis of remnants considered in this account to be Older Drift.

The recent survey shows the ice-margin to have been less lobate than Charlesworth's line. During maximum advance the margin of the thick ice lay only slightly farther east in the valleys of the Wye and the Wellington Brook than on the interfluves around hills such as Burghill (136 m above OD) and the Dinmore mass (227 m above OD). Within the marginal zone the drift fill-line suggests that the surface of the ice was inclined eastwards at between 2 and 3° for several kilometres. The most easterly lobe crossed the Lugg valley near Leominster from the broad lowland now occupied by the River Arrow to the west, and rose eastwards to between 115 and 130 m above OD. The maximum height of the ice-margin of the northern part of the same lobe to the west of the Orleton Moraine (Figure 19) (Luckman, 1960, p.203) appears to have been at 121 to 137 m.

The advancing ice overran a landscape that had suffered periglacial conditions throughout much of the Devensian, when extensive sheets of unconsolidated solifluction deposits must have formed on the slopes and filled the valleys. The ice removed this material and incorporated it, along with any remaining Older Drift or River Terrace gravels, into its subglacial sediment load. The Newer Drift, therefore, contains clasts of local Old Red Sandstone calcretes and sandstones in addition to farther travelled erratics. The latter are predominantly westerly derived and include Ludlow sandstones and siltstones, probable Llandovery greywacke sandstones associated with white vein-quartz, less common

Silurian limestones, debris from the Townsend Tuff Bed, cornstone conglomerates, and volcanic rocks probably from around Builth (Curley, 1863, p.179; Pocock, 1925, pp.21–22). In the north of the district greywacke is less common, and Ludlow material becomes dominant over Old Red Sandstone debris in the north-west. Hanter's Hill Gabbro is recorded only from the north.

The present geomorphology of the district has been governed partly by the depositional effects of the Devensian ice, but probably more by glacial erosion. The valleys were widened and deepened by ice action. Several minor dry or misfit meltwater channels date from the closing phase of glaciation, and at this time the Wye established a new course through the Breinton gorge due to the blockage of its old channel at Stretton Sugwas [463 428]. Periglacial action in unglaciated areas probably also contributed significantly to erosion.

### Newer Till

This till occurs as a thin blanket, forming a smooth, undulating, subdued landscape. It consists predominantly of slightly reddish brown, clayey to sandy silt, with unsorted clasts commonly up to small cobble grade, but including rarer larger cobbles and boulders. The clasts exhibit a wide range of roundness, and ice-polishing, smoothing and faceting are characteristic; striations are common on the fine-grained Ludlow sandstones. Most of the deposit is probably an ablation till, deposited during deglaciation from debris bands spread along thrust planes in the ice or from supraglacial debris. In the west, e.g. in the Yarsop area [410 478], and north of Garnons Hill [4078 4495], a stiffer, redder, more clayey deposit is probably subglacial lodgement till, but its extent is uncertain as elsewhere it is probably mostly covered by ablation till. The two till types have not been distinguished on the map.

Over most of the area till, generally less than 4 m thick, rests directly on bedrock. On the low ground, however, it is thicker with kettle-holes and passes into hummocky kettle-kame moraines in the valleys. In some places, as along the proto-Wye from Stretton Sugwas to Hereford, till overlies fluvioglacial gravels where the advancing glacier overran outwash deposits emerging at the ice-front. Till has probably been removed by solifluction from the steeper scarp slopes though some hills carry a thin deposit near their tops, e.g. the Dinmore Hill mass has ice-marginal patches up to 233 m above OD.

In the wide, low-lying tract around Pembridge [390 580], Dilwyn [415 547] and Weobley [403 515], the till-moraine has a definite grain with subdued ridges trending west-south-west–east-north-east, parallel with the Aymestrey escarpment to the north. These were probably produced by ice moving towards the east-north-east. Other notable examples of such ridges occur between Pembridge and Barewood [c.390 570].

### End moraine

End moraines generally form ridges lying roughly north–south, subparallel with the former ice margin, and comprise poorly sorted cobbly gravel with silts and sands and some till. Their formation is attributed to periods of still-stand of sufficient duration for the accumulation of a significant deposit by melting or ablation at the ice-margin.

The Devensian terminal moraine, which may also be partly of ice-push origin, runs as a cobbly gravel ridge northwards from near Hereford racecourse [497 410], where 1.5 m of till were exposed in an excavation on its top, to the south-west flank of Burghill, where it laps against the Older Drift (Figure 14). At Tillington [470 465], it forms two cobbly gravel ridges associated with kettle holes. To the north-west, patches mapped as end moraine as far as Badnage [461 465] are thought to represent the ice-margin during an early stage of regression. Farther north the terminal moraine is manifest as a 400 m-long cobbly ridge climbing up the southern flank [494 490] of Derndale Hill, north of Wellington. Thence it continues in very subdued form over the Dinmore Hill mass, producing an arcuate train of thin till patches as far as Newton [510 540] in the Lugg valley. South-east of Leominster [530 580] (Figure 21C) the terminal moraine forms a belt of poorly sorted pebbly gravels, silts and sands, more than 12 m thick. North of Leominster it has been traced (Luckman, 1970, p.180) to the arcuate Orleton Moraine [500 665] (Dwerryhouse and Miller, 1930, p.112; Cross and Hodgson, 1975, p.321) which crosses the wide flat of the old Teme–Onny valley.

The Staunton Moraine (Aldis, 1905, p.327; Pocock, 1940, p.104; Luckman, 1970, p.185; Palmer, 1972, pp.7 and 8) on the western margin of the district runs northwards through Norton Canon [380 475] to Hyatt Sarnesfield [380 500]. Marking a major still-stand, it is a distinct flat-topped ridge up to 30 m high and 1 km wide. To the north the ice-margin may be represented by a ridge of gravel with kettle holes at Park Barn [410 530]. The main part of the Staunton Moraine is composed of poorly sorted gravels with silts and sands; up to 10 m are poorly exposed in the railway cutting [381 473] at Norton Canon. East of the moraine, the parallel Maddle Brook probably originated as an ice-marginal channel. Farther east a narrower morainic belt, 2 km long and 300 m wide, laps around the steep western buttress of Burton Hill [396 488] at 130 to 160 m above OD. This belt marks an earlier still-stand than the Staunton one, when Burton Hill had been freed of ice. It may continue northwards as patches of gravelly moraine at Park Barn or Swanstone Court [440 530]. The Burton Hill moraine was considered by Charlesworth (1929, p.348, pl.21) and Luckman (1970, p.182) to mark an embayment in the terminal moraine (Figure 19). Between Burton Hill and Burghill patchy and minor gravelly ridges, as at Yarsop [413 473] and Badnage [460 465], may represent positions of brief still-stand. A morainic ridge probably of similar origin runs north-west–south-east for about 1 km to the north-west of Stretton Sugwas [463 430]. This is 100 m wide and 10 m high and composed of gravelly clayey silt with stones and boulders.

## Kettle-kame moraine

This heterogeneous group of genetically related deposits (Price, 1973, p.138; Francis, 1975) occurs in valleys where the piedmont ice was thickest and below scarps where the ice lay mostly in shadow. In both situations the ice tended to remain as stagnant decaying masses during deglaciation and became engulfed by a mixture of tills, outwash gravels and ponded laminated silts. Deposits were laid down by meltwaters running under, within and against the ice, and as it melted, these were progressively deformed, thus eventually producing the disorderly moundy kame and kettle topography typical of the Wye valley above Stretton Sugwas [460 425]. The positions of former masses of dead ice are now marked by kettle holes up to 10 m deep. In places the hollows, commonly ponded, are interconnected by seepage lines through the drift deposits or are linked by marshy channels containing small misfit streams. These channels were probably eroded during or immediately after the melt by subglacial or proglacial streams. The hollows are separated by a network of kame ridges.

The moundy kame-complex of the Wye valley grades imperceptibly into smooth till terrain. The lowest part of the deposit is in the channel floor of the preglacial proto-Wye (Figure 20), which may locally have been deepened by subglacial erosion so that the kettled drift could be up to about 30 m thick. Small exposures occur at incised bends along the Wye, notably in the 15 m cliff at Old Weir [446 414]. Clarke (1949) described a partly faulted gravel sequence formerly exposed in a pit at Byford [3980 4294]. The best sections are in the Stretton Sugwas gravel pits [c.455 423], up to about 20 m deep (Symonds, 1862, p.134; Aldis, 1905, p.328; Moore, 1905, p.331; Richardson, 1911, p.66; Pocock, 1925, p.21; 1940, pp.105–106; Grindley, 1954, pp.37–40; Luckman, 1970, pp.182–183). The deformation of the beds is general (Plate 8), but varies enormously in degree. Large-scale recumbent isoclinal folding occurs at Stretton Sugwas [4500 4235]. The random orientation of the folds suggests that they are mostly ice-contact features due to deposition against, or on, ablating ice, though some of the lowest gravels may well be earlier outwash deformed by the main ice-advance.

A basal lodgement till occurs in places beneath the kettle-kame moraine at Stretton Sugwas (Aldis, 1905; Moore, 1905), and in the western and northern pits the moraine is buried beneath sandur outwash and alluvium. The kettle-kame moraine fills the proto-Wye channel and is here up to 17.5 m thick. The steep southern side of the ancient valley [4553 4202], formed of mudstone overlain by a thin till, was exposed during excavations in 1981. A subglacial channel, 200 to 250 m wide and up to 6 m deep, was proved in test borings beneath the graded channel floor, and is filled with red-brown silt containing a few pebbles (Figure 20). The overlying kettle-kame moraine comprises stratified, immature, imbricated, fluvioglacial gravels with thin beds of red-brown silt and sand, and gradational, interbedded, gravelly ablation tills. The tills seem to be commoner in the upper part of the sequence, alongside thickish beds of highly contorted, laminated silts (rhythmites), with layers of stony flow tills (Plate 8). Palaeocurrents deduced from clast imbrication at Stretton Sugwas are aligned along the proto-Wye channel towards the east and north-east. Grindley (1954, p.40) recorded teeth of the woolly rhinoceros (*Coelodonta antiquitatis*) and mammoth (*Mammuthus primigenius*) from the pits, although their exact provenance is uncertain.

North of the Wye valley there is a small area of kettle moraine with sand pits at Bishopstone [c.416 442]. About

**Plate 8**   Slumped laminated silts and tills in kettle-kame moraine, Stretton Sugwas gravel pits [4573 4222].

The lowest deposit is probably an ablation till composed of unsorted subangular to rounded Lower Palaeozoic sandstone clasts arranged chaotically in a reddish brown silt matrix. The laminated beds (rhythmites) above indicate ponding and contain seasonal layers of pale reddish brown sand-silt alternating with darker clay-silt laminae. Thin pebbly layers were probably produced by slumping of the till (A13299)

24 m of sand and gravel are recorded in a borehole nearby [4133 4339].

## Glacial Sand and Gravel

In the northern part of the district several moundy patches on the till plain consist of cross-bedded, moderately sorted, immature gravels with lenses of sand.

A moundy area of sand and gravel near Dilwyn [417 545] contains a large kettle hole south of the village, and has been worked from a pit 7 m deep on its south-east side [4206 5437], where 3.5 m of thickly bedded, fairly well-sorted gravel with thin beds of sand are exposed. Most of the deposit may be related genetically to kettle-kame moraine, but its extension along Stretford Brook may be entirely fluvioglacial.

A large area of ill-sorted gravels with sand lenses at Stretford [440 560] has bedding inclined at 30 to 45° to the south-west and has a ridged topography corresponding to the north-west–south-east strike of beds. These are best exposed in a pit [4387 5617] where they are cut by several faults. The sediments are partially cemented adjacent to the faults and the clasts commonly have a calcite efflorescence throughout. The steep dip cannot be a primary depositional feature, and its direction is opposite to that expected from the effects of ice-movement from the west: penecontemporaneous slumping is possible though it is suspected from the partial cementation and general dearth of Welsh greywacke clasts that these gravels may be Older Drift deposits disturbed by the later glaciation (p.33). A short transverse ridge mapped as Glacial Sand and Gravel [447 547] near Bucknell consists of cobbly gravel in a pit, and may possibly be end-moraine.

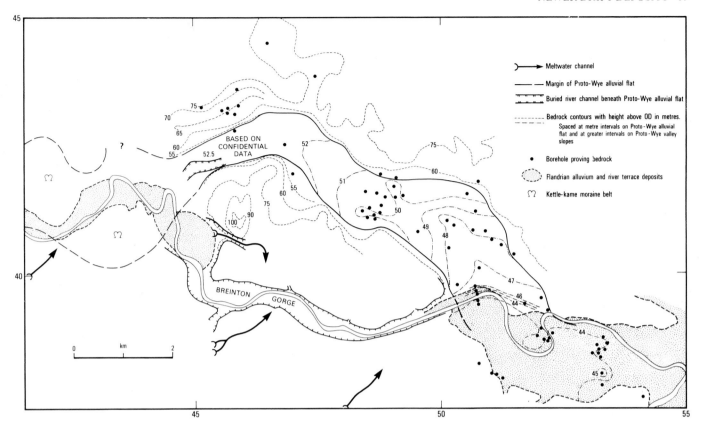

**Figure 20** Rock-head contours along the Proto-Wye alluvial flat from Stretton Sugwas to Hereford City

Ridges trending east-north-east–west-south-west at Monkland [455 575] and Ivington Bury [473 568] lie roughly normal to the local ice front, suggesting a kamiform or esker-like origin. The Monkland deposit, at least 9 m thick in a borehole [4525 5742], consists mostly of gravel, with stony and stoneless silt. The more subdued Ivington Bury ridge contains a kettle hole, and a 5 m-deep pit [4748 5687] shows flat-lying, cross-bedded and imbricated gravels deposited by stream flow from the west.

### Newer Fluvioglacial Terrace Deposits

Fluvioglacial sediments were deposited by meltwater at all stages of the glaciation. As the ice-sheet advanced, subglacial rivers emerged at the glacial snout and deposited spreads of sand and gravel as valley sandar, well beyond the ice-margin, some of which may have been eventually overridden by ice. The deposits proved in the many boreholes along the proto-Wye channel below Stretton Sugwas (Figure 20) were probably formed in this way. They are covered by till to the west of the ice-margin near Hereford.

As the climate ameliorated and the ice-sheet retreated, torrential meltwater reworked debris in the valleys to form sandar which extended across much of the low ground. Beneath the modern alluvium these deposits floor most of the valleys from the Lugg westwards, and they merge eastwards with similar gravels formed under the influence of periglaciation.

In continuity with the suballuvial gravels there are marginal terrace-benches that vary in height from about 0.5 to 4 m above the present floodplain, and locally up to 10 m at the terrace-back. The benches are usually capped by 1.5 to 3 m of sandy silt, containing a few pebbles in the lower part, that has been included with the Fluvioglacial Terrace Deposits.

Other fluvioglacial spreads bear little or no relationship to existing valleys, but originate at former ice-marginal positions over hilly terrain where meltwater drained by the most direct route to leave fans and drapes of sand and gravel.

The gravels are immature, reddish brown, sandy and generally well stratified. The degree of coarseness varies considerably and the clasts are similar to those of the Devensian till. Because of the interest engendered by their use as aquifers or sources of aggregate, thicknesses are fairly well documented along the proto-Wye channel (Hardy and Young, 1973 and 1975), where they are 5 to 8 m thick west of the ice-margin, and 7.5 to 10 m thick proglacially at Hereford. Temporary excavations beneath Hereford City [5009 4027; 5077 4050] have yielded easterly palaeocurrent readings (108° and 092° respectively). In the Lugg valley the gravels thin southwards from 10 to 13.5 m in the Newton [512 540] area to 4 to 7.5 m at Bodenham [530 510] and 3.6 to 5.3 m at Lugg Bridge [530 417]. The thickness of fluvioglacial gravel beneath alluvium is uncertain, and generally less than the gravel thickness recorded in boreholes, for the upper layers are probably alluvial gravel. Elsewhere thickness records are unreliable.

A complete 6 m-thick sequence through a broad fluvio-glacial fan in the Yazor Brook valley, emanating from the Brinsop valley, has been exposed recently in the western-most pits at Stretton Sugwas [c.447 423]. The fan overlies kettle-kame moraine, and consists of 2.3 m of sand and silt overlain by up to 1.6 m of coarse pebbly sand, capped by up to 3 m of sandy gravel; the depositional currents flowed to the east (090° to 112°). The deposit is overlain by 1.5 m of silty alluvium.

Upstream from the constricted Yazor Brook alluvial chan-nel at Kenchester, the 1.5 km-wide former lacustrine flat of Brinsop Common [428 443] (Pocock, 1940, p.106) is under-lain by outwash gravels.

There are several records of water-rolled vertebrate re-mains from the fluvioglacial gravels, including molars of mammoth (*M. primigenius*) and straight-tusked elephant (*Palaeoloxodon antiquus*) from below Hereford Infirmary [c.516 401] and the molar of the woolly rhinoceros (*C. anti-quitatis*) probably from a gravel pit in the Lugg gravels near Dinmore station [5135 5030] (Curley, 1867a, p.170; 1887, p.248; Symonds, 1872, p.223; 1889, pp.22 and 24). The straight-tusked elephant remains, if correctly identified, are likely to be derived from an interglacial deposit.

## Head and fluvioperiglacial (periglacial sandar) gravels

During the latter part of the Devensian stage the area beyond the ice-margin underwent prolonged, and occasionally severe, periglaciation (Worsley, 1977). This gave rise to the local head deposits, formed by solifluction (or gelifluction) of seasonally thawed oversaturated surface layers over im-permeable permanently frozen substrata (Dines and others, 1940). Because of their similarity it is rarely possible to separate head *senso stricto* and colluvium (see p.41) in the field.

Where solid rocks are the parent sources, head normally consists of angular fragments of rock, derived from up-slope, embedded in a sandy silt matrix; where the source is partly or wholly glacial drift, the head is similar to till in appearance being generally structureless or only crudely stratified. Though it can be thick at the foot of steep slopes, solifluction has carried the material onto quite gentle slopes where it forms feather edges or has been reworked by flood washing (see below). It has been delineated only where consistently at least 1 m thick and of significant areal extent.

The most extensive head deposit in the district forms a wide apron mantling the northern slopes of the Woolhope Dome. It consists of up to 3 m of yellow-buff to brown sandy silt with abundant angular rock fragments from the Ludlow and the Rushall Formation. It has built up a long altiplana-tion terrace that grades into the alluvial flat of the Frome. Small flows of similar head occur around Shucknall Hill. Unlike elsewhere these deposits are conspicuous by the col-our contrast with the underlying Raglan Mudstone.

Largely coeval with the fluvioglacial outwash sheets, and partly merging with them, are very similar gravels forming periglacial sandar to the east of the Lugg and, therefore, beyond direct glacial influence. These aggradations floor the valleys of the Little Lugg, Frome, the Lodon and its old abandoned course westwards to the Lugg, and most of the minor valleys in this part of the district. They originated as periglacial mudflows which were reworked by seasonal fluviatile wash throughout the Devensian, and especially around and immediately after the time of the main ice-retreat when tundra conditions prevailed (Penny, 1974, pp.259–260). The gravels are mainly silty and contain few pebbles larger than 3 cm across. The clasts are predominant-ly calcrete nodules, together with up to 20 per cent of sand-stones from the Old Red Sandstone and minor amounts of Ludlow sandstones and vein-quartz derived from the solifluction of the Older Drift.

Usually only 0.5 to 1.5 m of the gravels are seen beneath alluvial silt in stream banks; their total thickness is in most cases uncertain but is probably less than 3 m. Furthermore their upper parts are likely to have been affected by Fla-ndrian fluvial reworking. Between Yarkhill and Stretton Grandison [621 431] the gravels crop out marginally to the Frome alluvium, and were once worked from small pits. Gravels were proved to 11.3 m in a nearby well [6280 4348]. Similar gravels, 8 m thick in a well [6150 4390], floor the abandoned misfit Lodon channel at Monkhide, and 1.5 m of partially cemented gravel is exposed at the truncated end of its abandoned course at Monksbury Court [6187 4395].

Around Pool Head [555 505] in the Lugg valley a flat ex-panse is underlain by at least 7 m of similar fine gravels. They have been worked to a depth of 4 m [5520 5070].

During the construction of the Hereford and Gloucester Canal mammal bones and teeth were discovered in these gravels, mainly along Stony Brook, near Bosbury, at the eastern margin of the district [662 414] eastwards for 1.6 km (Anon, 1907, p.4; Scobie, 1907, pp.14–15). The fauna is recorded as mammoth, elk, deer and possibly hippopoto-mus, bison and hog but is unconfirmed in detail.

Small-scale periglacial disturbances affect the surface layers of all but the Flandrian gravels. The uppermost 1.5 to 2 m of gravel in pits is commonly till-like due to a combina-tion of silt enrichment by downward infiltration and car-bonate leaching; the elongate clasts in it have been vertically reorientated, and the more fissile lithologies show signs of splitting. The disruption is assumed to have occured during the Devensian. Ice-wedge casts have been recorded in the Older fluvioglacial gravels at Blackwardine and Windmill Hill and from the Sutton Walls Terrace gravels at Sutton Walls [524 464] (Luckman, 1970, p.191).

## Glacial erosion, river diversion and meltwater drainage channels

Devensian glacial and periglacial erosion profoundly affected the geomorphology of the district. Erosion was enhanced at the glacial margins, where the relatively high ice velocity and temperate basal ice conditions maximised the horizontal traction force on subglacial materials (Boulton and others, 1977, pp.231 and 240). The advancing ice plucked at the soft mudstone flanks of the hills and widened the valleys. This widening continued on deglaciation by the erosion of oversteepened slopes. Such wide, misfit, valleys as that of the Wellington Brook [488 482], and that between Tillington Common [468 458] and Moreton on Lugg [510 460] prob-ably formed in this way. The contrast between the plateau country of the St Maughans Formation, which lay east of the ice, and the broken landscape of isolated steep tabular hills

The following stages are represented:

A   Pre-Older Drift
B   Post-Older Drift–Pre-Newer Drift
C   Maximum extent of Newer Drift ice margin
D   Early Regressive stage of Newer Drift ice margin
E   Present

Stretford Brook is also referred to as Cheaton Brook

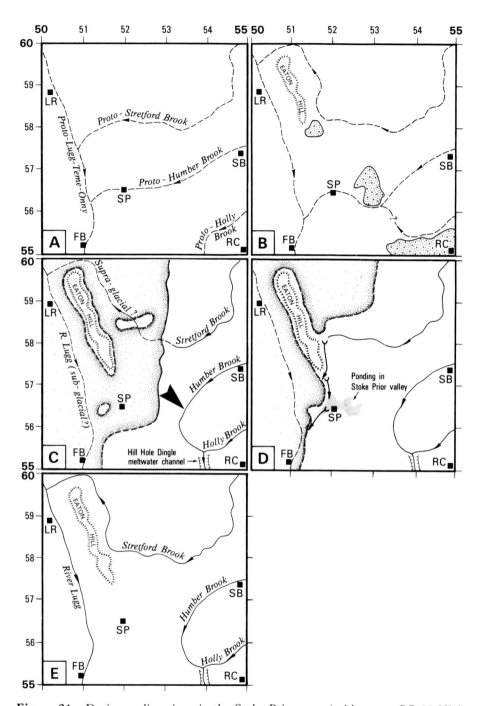

Figure 21   Drainage diversions in the Stoke Prior area (grid square SO 55 NW)

Meltwater channel

Outwash fan

Maximum extent of Devensian ice

Older Drift filling channels

Abbreviations:

LR   Leominster railway station
SP   Stoke Prior church
FB   Ford Bridge
RC   Risbury Cross
SB   Steen's Bridge

separated by wide flat-bottomed valleys of the glaciated region may well have been intensified by glacial erosion. This agency produced such forms as the peculiar conical hills of the area around King's Pyon [438 507] and Canon Pyon [462 488]. The hills of the glaciated region appear 'stream-lined' in a fashion suggesting ice-movement mainly to the south-east in the south and to the north-east in the north with Westhope Hill as the point of divergence.

Major diversions of drainage by the Devensian ice affected the Lugg and the Wye. In the north, eastward-moving ice eventually blocked the course of the Teme and the Onny, diverting them eastwards to the Severn (Pocock, 1925, p.32; Dwerryhouse and Miller, 1930, pp.123–125; Cross and Hodgson, 1975).

Aldis (1905 p.328) was the first to point out that the original course of the Wye was from Stretton Sugwas [460 425] to Hereford, along a line close to the present Yazor Brook. This latter stream is a misfit flowing through a broad flat tract floored by till and fluvioglacial gravels, and rock-head contours derived from the many boreholes through this aquifer show the graded proto-Wye channel beneath the tract (Figure 20). The present Wye bypasses this stretch along the Breinton gorge cut largely through solid rock from Lower Eaton [445 405] to Broomy Hill [496 393]. The Wye shows no signs of having been ponded back upriver from the gorge, the new course probably being superimposed from that of a supraglacial river during an early stage of the glacial retreat when the ice-front ran from Lower Eaton to Stretton Sugwas and formed the end moraine north-west of that village. A now completely dry meltwater channel between Sugwas Court [455 408] and Upper Breinton [463 407] was in use about this time, when the proto-Wye channel at Stretton Sugwas was presumably blocked by glacial debris and large masses of decaying ice. The westerly continuation of the meandering proto-Wye can be discerned from Byford to Canon Bridge by the outcrop of thick kettle-kame moraine (Figure 20), and it is just upriver from this stretch that the modern river again significantly departs from its preglacial route, where this was blocked by the Staunton Moraine (p.37). The proto-Wye channel is believed to have passed Staunton on Wye between Oaker's Hill and Garnons Hill, for rockhead as low as 50 m above OD was proved in a well [3673 4526]. An alternative course north of Garnons Hill suggested by Pocock (1940, p.104) and Palmer (1972, p.11) is not confirmed.

In the northern part of the district, ice crossed the Lugg valley south of Leominster, and probably diverted the Humber and Holly brooks. Dwerryhouse and Miller (1930, p.113) claimed that these originally flowed to the short 'dry' Stoke Prior valley [523 566], and supposed that this course was blocked by ice and glacial debris which diverted the brooks southwards to cut a deep narrow gorge (Hill Hole Dingle) through Older Drift into solid rock from Risbury [540 554] to Hampton Court [521 526] (Figure 21B, C).

The incised nature of the Dinmore meander compared with the very broad open Lugg valley to the south has led to suggestions that it originated as a meltwater channel diversion of the last glaciation (Grindley, 1918, p.229; 1954, p.43; Dwerryhouse and Miller, 1930, pp.113–114) or an earlier glaciation (Luckman, 1970, p.180) and a variety of preglacial Lugg courses have been proposed. The presence of both Older Drift and river terraces within the Dinmore gorge show, however, that it is a very ancient feature as first postulated by Clarke (1934, p.42). Moreover, it is well known that the preservation of meander-shaped valleys is related to the resistance of the country rock (e.g. Drury, 1954, p.200) and the Lugg valley is broad and open over Raglan Mudstone and only confined to a meandering gorge where it cuts through the more resistant St Maughans Formation. The course of the Lugg is probably essentially part of a superimposed primary river pattern of Neogene age (George, 1974, p.367) and originated on the Low Peneplain at about 250 m above OD, represented by the St Maughans Formation plateau of the region (Brown, 1960, fig. 44).

Many of the valleys in the glaciated area are preglacial, but some were totally dependent on meltwater and are now gross misfits. There are good examples north of Stoke Prior associated with the Cheaton (or Stretford) Brook (Figure 21). These valleys were cut during an early regressive phase, when the ice had not cleared the lower part of the Cheaton valley [c.516 585] and still occupied the Lugg valley about Leominster. A dry channel [518 580] at 88 m above OD, only 4 m above the alluvium, was recognised by Dwerryhouse and Miller (1930, p.113) as an overflow channel; it took meltwater around the south-east end of the ice-free rock barrier of Eaton Hill towards Stoke Prior (Figure 21D). Here the water ponded against standing ice in the main Lugg channel to the west and deposited the fluvioglacial sand and gravel flat around Stoke Prior Church [520 565]. An overflow from this lake found an outlet at 78 m above OD [517 563] into the Lugg farther south. Luckman (1970, p.180) concluded that this was the original course of Cheaton Brook, which was diverted northward by advancing ice, but the presence of Devensian till in the present Cheaton Brook outlet confirms the view of Dwerryhouse and Miller that the brook flowed northward around Eaton Hill prior to the last glaciation. However, this channel seems to have been initiated by a diversion dating from the time of the Older Drift, since its original course, now buried beneath Older fluvioglacial gravel [c.515 580], was due west to the Lugg (Figures 10, 14 and 21B).

## FLANDRIAN DEPOSITS

### Postglacial Wye terraces

Along the Wye valley west of Hereford there are several terraces on the insides of bends. These were left as the river began to widen its flood plain across the area of kettle-kame moraine in postglacial times. The fronts of the terrace remnants vary from 1.5 to 3 m above the flood plain and the deposit consists of about 1 to 2 m of brown silt with some stones. These remnants are termed the 1st (or Stretton Sugwas) Terrace of the Wye; a second terrace, about 8 m above the alluvium, is found only in the Breinton gorge.

### Colluvium

Colluvium is hill-wash accumulated in quite recent times following deforestation and the spread of agriculture. It accumulates at the base of slopes, in hollows and on the upper sides of walls and hedges. Some of the more ancient field boundaries are marked by scarps 3 m high. Colluvium is thickest in minor lateral valleys in which streams have been culverted or piped. In areas underlain by the Raglan Mudstone it consists of brown sandy silt with fragments of calcrete and sandstone, but is more sandy over outcrops of the St Maughans Formation.

In the field it is difficult to distinguish between head and colluvium and it is rarely possible to separate the two. Boundaries with adjacent alluvium are transitional.

## Alluvium

Alluvium generally consists of a lower unit of sand and gravel, formed by fluvial traction, and an upper overbank unit of silt produced at times of flood from particles in suspension. In addition there are small deposits of lacustrine alluvium deposited in ponded water.

The two major drainage systems of the area, the Lugg and the Wye, have remarkably contrasting alluvial tracts. The River Lugg, in common with the Arrow, Frome and other major streams, has an alluvial flat that is wide in comparison to the size of the present river. This is partly because its course runs across readily eroded Raglan Mudstone, partly because the old valley floor was covered by thick fluvioglacial or fluvioperiglacial deposits, and partly because the Lugg was once a larger river (p.34). The 2 km-wide expanse of the fertile Lugg Meadows about the Lugg-Frome-Wye confluences near Hereford prompted Murchison (1839, pp.550–551) to suggest that it was once a lake, an hypothesis that held sway for much of the nineteenth century (Symonds, 1861b; Merewether, 1887b, p.21). The floodplain of the Wye, which has approximately four times the present average discharge of the Lugg (Hardy, 1972), has in contrast a fluvial channel only 200–600 m wide. This is accounted for by its youthfulness, since the preglacial proto-Wye channel was over 1 km wide (Figure 20).

Further differences between the Wye and the other rivers are equally striking. The Wye alluvium, 4 to 5 m thick, is pale buff-brown silt mostly derived from the Silurian rocks of central Wales. The basal gravel lag deposit is either thin or absent. Moreover, the river has cut down to rockhead between Preston on Wye and Hereford, and pavements of rock are visible in the bed during the summer. In the Arrow, Frome and most of the minor streams, especially in the Lugg, the alluvial silt and river bed are floored by a substantial thickness of gravel. There is little information on the nature and thickness of the alluvial gravels beneath the overbank silts for they cannot readily be distinguished from underlying fluvioglacial or fluvioperiglacial gravels. Possibly the top 0.5 to 1 m of gravel in most valleys has been reworked during Flandrian times. In the Lugg valley the overbank alluvium is approximately 3 m thick, and in other stream valleys 1 to 3 m are present. It is a homogeneous, soft, stoneless, finely sandy to clayey silt with a uniform reddish brown coloration derived from the Lower Old Red Sandstone in the upper part. The lower half is commonly variable in colour, being mottled brown and grey; it is blue-grey in the basal 0.3 m, probably due to the reducing properties of incorporated organic material.

The alluvial silt of Yazor Brook at Hereford is about 1.3 m thick, and varies greatly in colour, probably due to the former presence of interbedded peat. Before its artificial containment the Yazor was a sluggish stream flowing across a broad marshy area. Several sections through its alluvium were compiled, mainly during the construction of the Hereford sewers, by Curley (1858, 1863, 1867b) and Moore (1905).

Mammalian remains have been discovered in the alluvium. Red deer and aurochs are recorded from the Lugg alluvium (Symonds, 1872, pp.222–223; Curley, 1880, p.248) from Bodenham [5183 5123], and from the Wye alluvium at Hereford (Grindley, 1921, p.vi). The Yazor alluvium has yielded bones of ox, deer, horse (Moore, 1905, p.332) and goat (Curley, 1867b, pp.253–254). Rich molluscan and insect faunas are recorded from the basal alluvial deposits of the Yazor [c.5165 4034] (Curley, 1867b) and the Lugg [5129 4468; 5183 5123]. Two former records of foraminiferal 'marine clay' in the banks of the River Wye above Hereford have not been verified by recent work (Sumbler and others, 1985).

An interesting example of Flandrian river capture is provided by the Lodon and Frome valleys near Monksbury Court [619 439]. The Lodon is now diverted southwards for about 1.4 km into the Frome, whereas formerly it flowed westwards for 7 km to join the Little Lugg and eventually the Lugg, at Withington. The engineers of the old Gloucester–Hereford Canal exploited this 'dry' abandoned channel along its entire length. The width of the old alluvial flat is the same as the width of the Lodon channel upriver from the point of capture, and there is an abrupt fall of about 2.5 m at Monksbury Court, from the eastern end of the abandoned flat at about 66 m above OD, to the present-day Lodon floodplain. The Lodon's unusual former course was possibly established during the Older Drift glaciation.

Pond alluvium occupies many of the kettle holes, especially those in the kettle-kame moraine of the Wye valley. The silt has generally been reduced to a pale grey colour by former peat. A larger area of probable lacustrine alluvium (Pocock, 1940, p.106) occurs beneath Brinsop Common [427 443]. At least 2.5 m of pale brown to pink-brown clayey silt have been proved. Alluvium of a supposedly impounded former lake (Merewether, 1887b, p.22; Palmer, 1972, p.12) occurs to the west of the Staunton Moraine [377 475 and 377 460].

## Peat

Peat was once widespread in the district, but intensive drainage schemes and modern agricultural methods have led to its removal at all but a few sites. Many of the broad alluvial and fluvioglacial flats were formerly rough peaty areas, poorly drained by sluggish meandering streams, and now readily identified by toponyms such as 'moss', 'venn', 'fen', 'moor', 'marsh' or 'common'. At former peat sites the alluvial silts, normally red-brown or buff-brown, have commonly been bleached to pale greys or blue-greys. Borehole records and sewage excavations at Hereford (Curley, 1867b; Moore, 1905) show that beds of peat up to 1.5 m thick occur at several levels within the Yazor Brook alluvium. In addition peat formerly covered some of the hill-slopes, and apparently even as late as the mid-nineteenth century a blanket of peat extended from the Yazor alluvium on to the higher ground of much of the City area (Curley, 1858). ·

The most substantial accumulation of peat, over 1.3 m thick, floors an irregular north-west – south-east linear hollow near Tyberton in the extreme south-west of the district. The hollow was formed by the linking of a string of kettle holes in late glacial times, and is now poorly drained by a southern tributary stream of the Wye. Many of the small individual kettle holes in this part of the district are peaty or formerly contained peat.

## Landslip

Landslips are uncommon in the district. On steep scarps and in steep valleys in the Leominster – Bromyard plateau there have been landslips within the outcrop of the St Maughans Formation, probably associated with low downslope dips. Groundwater seepage from pervious layers of calcrete, sandstone and conglomerate weakens and lubricates the underlying mudstones and in wet weather the increase in porewater pressure may cause movement. The largest slip forms a belt 1.3 km long [567 517] on the south side of Dudale's Hope valley. There are minor slips on the north side of Hegdon Hill [5832 5427], on the south side of the Humber valley [5545 5726] and below Westhope Wood [454 514; 456 513]. The last two examples occur in the Raglan Mudstone Formation.

Another form of failure occurs on dip slopes along the periphery of the Woolhope Dome, where relatively steep dips parallel the hill slopes. Slab failure may take place along the thin bentonitic clays present in the Aymestry Limestone and Upper Ludlow Siltstone. The most notable example is 'The Slip' at Dormington [5918 4000] (Anon, 1907b; see Frontispiece), which occurred as a single abrupt movement on 15 March 1844, and was reported in the Hereford Journal of 20 March. The Slip is 290 m long and up to 80 m wide, consisting of a jumbled mass of blocks of Aymestry Limestone up to about 5 m across. The back scarp, about 120 m long, still provides one of the best local sections in the formation. Similar slab failure occurred in 1979 in the working Perton quarry, 250 m to the east of The Slip (Kendrick, 1979).

The River Wye is actively widening its channel above Hereford, and there are small movements on undercut river banks. These include small rotational slips in kettle-kame moraine near Bridge Sollers [415 419] and small rock-falls in the Raglan Mudstone, an old and stable example occurring near Sugwas Court [4535 4020].

# SEVEN

# Economic geology

Small excavations formerly worked for building stone, aggregate, brick- and tile-clay and lime, mostly for local use, are common. Their locations and purpose are shown on 1:10 560 ordnance maps of the last century and on the 1:10 000 geological sheets of this survey. Modern mineral working is now confined mainly to the quarrying of the Aymestry Limestone at Perton [5953 3993] and the extraction of gravel from the glacial and fluvioglacial deposits at Stretton Sugwas [450 425] and Bodenham [520 513].

## FULLER'S EARTH

Murchison (1839, pp.204,435) noted that fuller's earth was extracted for cleaning purposes from the Ludlow rocks, mainly on Shucknall Hill. The exact location is not known, but the material may have been a by-product of stone quarrying, since the bentonitic beds were probably thin. Squirrell and Tucker (1960, p.146) mention impersistent bentonite-like beds of grey or brown clay, up to 0.15 m thick, in the Aymestry Limestone of the Woolhope area.

## BRICK- AND TILE-CLAY

The main sources of brick- and tile-clay were the silty mudstones of the Lower Old Red Sandstone, although colluvium seems to have been used occasionally, for example near Hope under Dinmore [5050 5212]. The sites of small pits are scattered across the district, but around Hereford larger pits were opened in the 19th and early 20th centuries. Moore (1905, p.333) referred to one [518 421], now infilled, at Burcott, Holmer, that was used for brick-, tile- and pipe-making, and there is still a tile-works in operation adjacent to the disused canal, though the raw material is now imported . Pits also existed along the Ledbury Road at Tupsley, Hampton Park [527 397], and Barons Cross, Leominster. The Linton Tile Works [6671 5388], east of Bromyard, worked mudstones in the St Maughans Formation until comparatively recently.

## LIME

Lime-burning was formerly practised on a small scale, the principal raw material being the Bishop's Frome Limestone, though other mature calcretes of the Lower Old Red Sandstone were also used. The Bishop's Frome Limestone has been so exploited for lime or for aggregate (M'Cullough, 1869, p.8; Clarke, 1951, p.102) that much of its outcrop is marked by a narrow line of degraded pits. A sample from one such pit at Marlbrook [509 546] yielded 72 per cent calcium carbonate, and samples of calcretes from three lime-pits on the Leominster–Bromyard plateau contained 60 to 69 per cent (M'Cullough, 1869, p.9). The burnt lime was mainly used for mortar and as an agricultural dressing. The Hackley Limestone was worked at several places, but especially north-west and south-east of Hackley Farm [636 534]. Local lenses of cornstone conglomerate within the St Maughans Formation also seem to have had a high enough carbonate content for burning, as near Leasows [5388 5800]. Samples of the 4 to 8 mm fractions composed mostly of calcrete nodules from two pits [4849 4415; 4925 4471] in the Older Fluvioglacial Terrace gravels of the Burghill–Portway area contained 66 per cent calcium carbonate.

The less mature calcretes from the Raglan Mudstone and St Maughans formations were once pitted extensively as local sources of agricultural 'marl'. Clarke (1951, p.102) referred to hundreds of small, disused 'marl-pits' scattered over Garnons Hill. Lime-deficient fields were simply top-dressed with the untreated 'marl' as some are to this day.

## BUILDING STONE

The variegated sandstones of the Old Red Sandstone, known locally as 'Hereford Stone', make a warm, attractive building stone, although one that is generally not durable, probably because of its slight carbonate content. Small pits all over the district were worked for local buildings or rough wallstone. The more durable stones were used in the city of Hereford (Allen Howe, 1910, p.136) though the cathedral is built of Hollington Stone from the Staffordshire Trias (Watson, 1911, p.154). Withington Stone (Watson, 1911, p.265), a particularly coarse, brown, cross-bedded, pebbly 'grit' with rounded quartz pebbles, from the Withington syncline, is an unusually durable and superior stone. In the 19th century it was extensively quarried [e.g. 5623 4348] for the construction of prominent buildings such as Withington church and Withington Court. Symonds (1861a, p.231) refers to extensive quarries in red sandstone nearby at Lugwardine. Another sandstone of note was the drab, medium-grained Lyde Stone, quarried at Pipe and Lyde [5087 4350]. Garnstone was a similar rock from the St Maughans Formation quarried on the north-east side of Burton Hill [403 493] (Watson, 1911, p.264) and hard durable 'grits' in shades of pink and green were quarried for building stone on Garnons Hill (Clarke, 1951, p.102). Many of the parallel-laminated sandstones of the St Maughans Formation are fissile, making them useful for roofing and paving, and they have been quarried for this purpose on Garnons Hill (Clarke, 1951, p.102) and Dinmore Hill (Clarke, 1952, p.226). An example of their use can be seen in Mansell Grange church.

Substantial seams of cornstone conglomerate were worked for coarse building stone (M'Cullough, 1868, p.8) as at Barnstone Farm, Pencombe [5870 5338]. The Bishop's Frome Limestone is massive in places, and yielded a building stone on Credenhill (Allen Howe, 1910, p.186), which was adit-mined [4459 4485], and is also reported to have been worked underground at Bishop's Frome [6642 4870]. The hard sandstone layers in the Rushall Formation were pitted at Hagley and along the eastern side of Shucknall Hill, presumably for local building stone. Murchison (1854, p.135) reported that the Upper Ludlow Beds were much quarried for wallstone, but were very prone to weathering. They may also have been used as a flagstone or for roofing tiles. Many small pits occur in them at Shucknall Hill and around Stoke Edith, and were worked for rough building stone and road aggregate (Phillips, 1848, p.174).

## ROCK AGGREGATE

In the past, few hard stone beds were neglected as a source of aggregate for road or railway construction. Even in Murchison's day (1839, p.185) the Bartestree intrusion [567 405] had been much quarried; it had been virtually quarried away by the beginning of this century (Reynolds, 1908, p.501). The Bishop's Frome Limestone and other concretionary calcrete limestones of the Lower Old Red Sandstone make a natural, tough and durable aggregate suitable for roadmetal and repairs (M'Cullough, 1868, p.8); they were won at many places for this purpose such as on Garnons Hill (Clarke, 1951, p.102). The intraformational conglomerate lenses of the St Maughans Formation were also valued as roadstone (M'Cullough, 1868, p.8). Sandstones and hard siltstones of the Lower Old Red Sandstone were probably dug for aggregate over most of the district, especially for use in railway construction where located in proximity to the line, as on Credenhill (Symonds, 1872, p.227) and Lyde Hill [527 439]. The Aymestry Limestone was extensively quarried for roadmaking on Shucknall Hill (Murchison, 1839, p.435); it is still exploited at Perton Quarry [5953 3993], the aggregate having a variety of industrial purposes within a 50 km radius.

## SAND AND GRAVEL

The river terrace deposits are mature, well-sorted, sandy pebble-gravels with durable stones, particularly of Silurian sandstones, and thin sand lenses. The other gravels of the district are immature poorly sorted deposits with a high but variable proportion of clay, silt and sand. Their clasts, commonly up to cobble and boulder grade, are mostly of cornstones and friable sandstones which lessen their value and mainly render them fit for use only as low-grade fill.

### Older Fluvioglacial Terrace Deposits

Gravel pits, mostly disused, occur in several of the outcrops, the largest being at Sutton Hill [541 464] and Burghill–Portway [c.485 450] (Figures 14 and 15). The most important areas that might warrant future assessment are at Blackwardine [530 565], Risbury [c.540 540], Burghill–Portway and Stoke Hill [613 492].

### River terraces of the Lugg

The quality of these gravels is relatively good. The two lower terrace gravels rarely exceed 2 m, but exceptionally may reach 3 m, as in a former small pit in the 2nd Terrace [c.526 507] at Sutton St Michael (Richardson, 1935, p.60); 6 m of gravel of this terrace were proved in a well [5431 5125] at England's Gate. The 3rd Terrace remnant at Kingsfield was 3 m thick in a trial pit [5222 4989]. The thickest deposits are, however, those of the 4th Terrace. They have been quarried extensively at Sutton Walls [525 464] and Lugwardine–Bartestree [560 416], where they are 8 and 4 m thick respectively. The thickness of gravel on the east side of Sutton Walls has not been proved, and the Lugwardine site has largely been sterilised by housing.

### Glacial Sand and Gravel, and Newer Till

Several gravel pods within the Devensian till-plain have been pitted, for example near Dilwyn [420 550] and Ivington [4747 5686], and even the ablation till is gravelly enough locally to have been dug for local use, for example at Three Elms [4895 4237]. The distribution of gravel within the till is not generally known.

### End moraine

At a point [5320 5785] where it crosses the Stretford Brook valley, the Devensian terminal moraine has been pitted for sand and gravel to a depth of 12 m. It could be of future value for local use.

### Kettle-kame moraine

The kettle-kame deposit of the Wye valley west of Hereford contains one of the largest potential sand and gravel resources in the county. Along with the overlying fluvioglacial deposits, it is currently extracted on a large scale from faces up to 20 m high at Stretton Sugwas [c.455 421]. The gravel is washed and graded into fractions for a variety of uses. The deposit is very variable, being an assemblage of fluvioglacial sand and gravels, ablation tills and laminated silts and sands, so heterogeneous that it is impossible to be certain about thickness and quality over the unproved part of the main outcrop. Former small sand pits occur in similar material near Bishopstone [4150 4428].

### Newer Fluvioglacial Terrace Deposits

These deposits are continuous and extensive spreads of immature gravel with a uniform thickness. Because of the generally high water-table, the gravel is worked mainly by dredging which accounts for the dearth of old pits. The gravel contains a preponderance of clasts of local calcrete and sandstone, together with more durable Lower Palaeozoic greywackes and sandstones. There is large-scale working in the Lugg valley at Wellington [499 488] and, most importantly, at Bodenham [523 512]. The valley is underlain by a large potential resource of mainly untested gravel, up to 13.5 m thick in the north thinning to about 5 m in the south. The deposit is thickest beneath the terrace remnants adjoining the alluvium.

Analogous gravels in the Wellington Brook valley [c.490 485], the misfit valley west of Moreton on Lugg [c.490 465], the Arrow valley [c.400 587], and other places such as Stretton Sugwas, are also largely untested, but may contain valuable resources. The gravel in the Arrow valley north of Pembridge is extensive, and has been proved in a borehole [3952 5895] at Twyford to be 24 m thick. The deposit hereabouts comprises about 90 per cent relatively durable Ludlovian rocks, making this a particularly promising area for exploration.

## Fluvioperiglacial gravels

The gravels in the graded valleys east of the Lugg are essentially suballuvial and of local Lower Old Red Sandstone composition; because of the high water-table they have not been widely exploited. An exception is a deposit marginal to the Frome floodplain at Yarkhill [6210 4313]. A borehole [6280 4348] in this area proved 11 m of sand and gravel beneath alluvium. Similar gravels in the abandoned Lodon channel at Monkhide [615 439] are 7 m thick. Farther north it is probably these local gravels that have been worked dry to 4 m in a small excavation near Pool Head [5520 5069]. The full thickness of the large expanse of gravel hereabouts may be as much as 10 m.

## A GEOLOGICAL CODE OF CONDUCT

Please obey the Country Code. Remember to shut gates and leave no litter.

Always seek permission before entering private land. Enclose a stamped addressed envelope when asking to visit sites.

Don't litter fields or roads with rock fragments. If you have a geological hammer, use it sparingly; indiscriminate hammering damages outcrops for those who come after.

Avoid undue disturbance to wildlife.

Keep collecting to an absolute minimum. Better still, take your specimens away as photographs. If they are needed for bona-fide study, collect only from fallen blocks.

Beware of dangerous cliffs and rock faces. Wear safety helmets where advisable.

Before working in hill areas ensure that you are properly equipped, and inform someone of your intended route and estimated time of return.

# REFERENCES

ALDIS, T S. 1905. Drift in the Wye valley. *Trans. Woolhope Nat. Field Club,* (1904) Vol. for 1902–4, 325–329.

ALLEN, J R L. 1960. Cornstone. *Geol. Mag.,* Vol. 97, 43–48.

— 1963. The Downtonian and Dittonian facies of the Welsh Borderland. *Geol. Mag.,* Vol. 100, 129–155.

— 1964. Primary current lineation in the Lower Old Red Sandstone (Devonian), Anglo-Welsh basin. *Sedimentology,* Vol. 3, 89–108.

— 1974a. Studies in fluviatile sedimentation: implications of pedogenic carbonate units, Lower Old Red Sandstone, Anglo-Welsh outcrop. *Geol. J.,* Vol. 9, 181–207.

— 1974b. Sedimentology of the Old Red Sandstone (Siluro–Devonian) in the Clee Hills area, Shropshire, England. *Sediment. Geol.,* Vol. 12, 73–167.

— 1974c. The Devonian rocks of Wales and the Welsh Borderland. 47–84 in *The Upper Palaeozoic and post-Palaeozoic rocks of Wales.* OWEN T R (editor). 426pp. (Cardiff: University of Wales Press.)

— 1977. Wales and the Welsh Borders. 40–110 in A correlation of Devonian rocks of the British Isles. HOUSE, M R, RICHARDSON, J B, CHALONER, W G, ALLEN, J R L, HOLLAND, C H, and WESTOLL, T S. *Spec. Rep. Geol. Soc. London,* No. 8. 110pp.

— 1979. Old Red Sandstone facies in external basins, with particular reference to southern Britain. 65–80 in The Devonian System. HOUSE, M R, SCUTTON, C T, and BASSETT, M G (editors). *Spec. Pap. Palaeontol.,* No. 23. 353pp.

— 1983. Studies in fluviatile sedimentation: bars, bar-complexes and sandstone sheets (low-sinuosity braided streams) in the Brownstones (L. Devonian), Welsh Borders. *Sediment. Geol.,* Vol. 33, 237–293.

— 1985. Marine to fresh water: the sedimentology of the interrupted environmental transition (Ludlow–Siegenian) in the Anglo-Welsh region. *Philos. Trans. R. Soc. London,* Ser. B, Vol. 309, 85–104.

— and CROWLEY, S F. 1983. Lower Old Red Sandstone fluvial dispersal systems in the British Isles. *Trans. R. Soc. Edinburgh, Earth Sci.,* Vol. 74, 61–68.

— and DINELEY, D L. 1976. The succession of the Lower Old Red Sandstone (Siluro-Devonian) along the Ross–Tewkesbury Spur Motorway (M50), Hereford and Worcester. *Geol. J.,* Vol. 11, 1–14.

— and TARLO, L B. 1963. The Downtonian and Dittonian facies of the Welsh Borderland. *Geol. Mag.,* Vol. 100, 129–155.

— and WILLIAMS B P J. 1978. The sequence of the earlier Lower Old Red Sandstone (Siluro–Devonian), north of Milford Haven, southwest Dyfed (Wales). *Geol. J.,* Vol. 13, 113–136.

— — 1979. Interfluvial drainage on Siluro-Devonian alluvial plains in Wales and the Welsh Borders. *J. Geol. Soc. London,* Vol. 136, 361–366.

— — 1981a. Sedimentology and stratigraphy of the Townsend Tuff Bed (Lower Old Red Sandstone) in South Wales and the Welsh Borders. *J. Geol. Soc. London,* Vol. 138, 15–29.

— — 1981b. *Beaconites antarticus*: a giant channel-associated trace fossil from the Lower Old Red Sandstone of South Wales and the Welsh Borders. *Geol. J.,* Vol. 16, 255–269.

— — 1982. The architecture of an alluvial suite: rocks between the Townsend Tuff and Pickard Bay Tuff Beds (early Devonian), southwest Wales. *Philos. Trans. R. Soc. London,* Ser. B, Vol. 297, 51–89.

ALLEN HOWE, J. 1910. *The geology of building stones.* 455pp. (London: Edward Arnold.)

ANDERTON, R, BRIDGES, P H, LEEDER, M R, and SELLWOOD, B W. 1979. Dynamic stratigraphy of the British Isles. 301pp. (London: George Allen and Unwin Ltd.)

Anon. 1907a. *Trans. Woolhope Nat. Field Club* (1852), Vol. for 1852–65, 4.

— 1907b. The Dormington landslip. *Trans. Woolhope Nat. Field Club* (1857), Vol. for 1852–65, 190–191.

ARTHUR, M J. 1982. Investigations of geophysical anomalies in the Hereford area of the Welsh Borderland. *Rep. Appl. Geophys. Unit. Inst. Geol. Sci.,* No. 122. 196pp. [Unpublished.]

BADHAM, J P N. 1982. Strike-slip orogens—an explanation for the Hercynides. *J. Geol. Soc. London,* Vol. 139, 493–504.

BALL, H W, and DINELEY, D L. 1952. Notes on the Old Red Sandstone of the Clee Hills. *Proc. Geol. Assoc.,* Vol. 63, 207–214.

— — 1961. The Old Red Sandstone of Brown Clee Hill and the adjacent area. 1. Stratigraphy. *Bull. Br. Mus. (Nat. Hist.) Geol.,* Vol. 5, 177–242.

BASSETT, M G. 1984. Lower Palaeozoic Wales—a review of studies in the past 25 years. *Proc. Geol. Assoc.,* Vol. 95, 291–311.

— LAWSON, J D, and WHITE, D E. 1982. The Downton Series as the fourth series of the Silurian System. *Lethaia,* Vol. 15, 1–24.

BOULTON, G S, JONES, A S, CLAYTON, K M, and KENNING, M J. 1977. A British ice-sheet model and patterns of glacial erosion and deposition in Britain. 231–246 in *British Quaternary Studies: recent advances.* SHOTTON, F W (editor). 298pp. (Oxford: Clarendon Press.)

BOWEN, D Q. 1973. The Pleistocene history of Wales and the borderland. *Geol. J.,* Vol. 8, 207–224.

— ROSE, J, McCABE, A M, and SUTHERLAND, D G. 1986. Correlation of Quaternary glaciations in England, Ireland, Scotland and Wales. *Quaternary Sci. Rev.,* Vol. 5, 299–340.

BRANDON, A. 1988. *Geological notes and local details for 1:10 000 sheets*: SO 74 SW (Coddington). (Keyworth: British Geological Survey.)

— and HAINS, B A. 1981. *Geological notes and local details for 1:10 000 sheets*: SO 43 NE, SO 44 SE, S0 53 NW, SO 54 SW (Hereford City). (Keyworth: Institute of Geological Sciences.)

BRODIE, P B. 1869. On the occurrence of remains of *Eurypterus* and *Pterygotus* in the Upper Silurian rocks in Herefordshire. *Q. J. Geol. Soc. London,* Vol. 25, 235–237.

— 1871. On the 'Passage-Beds' in the neighbourhood of Woolhope, Herefordshire, and on the discovery of a new species of *Eurypterus*, and some new land-plants in them. *Q. J. Geol. Soc. London*, Vol. 27, 256–261.

BROWN, E H. 1960. *The relief and drainage of Wales.* 186pp. (Cardiff: University of Wales Press.)

BUCKLAND, W. 1821. Description of the Quartz Rock of the Lickey Hill in Worcestershire, and of the strata immediately surrounding it; …(etc.). *Trans. Geol. Soc. London*, Vol. 5, 506–544.

BURGESS, I C. 1960. Fossil soils of the Upper Old Red Sandstone of south Ayrshire. *Trans. Geol. Soc. Glasgow*, Vol. 24, 138–153.

BURNHAM, C P. 1965. The soils of Herefordshire. *Trans. Woolhope Nat. Field Club*, Vol. 38, 27–35.

CALEF, C E, and HANCOCK, N J. 1974. Wenlock and Ludlow marine communities in Wales and the Welsh Borderland. *Palaeontology*, Vol. 17, 779–810.

CATT, J A. 1981. British pre-Devensian glaciations. 9–19 in *The Quaternary in Britain.* NEALE, J, and FLENLEY, J (editors). 267pp. (Oxford: Pergamon Press.)

CHADWICK, R A. 1985. Province inversion and basin subsidence as a result of compressional and extensional tectonics in the Worcester Basin. Meeting of the Joint Association for Geophysics, Geological Society of London.

— 1985. Introduction. 1–5 in *Atlas of onshore sedimentary basins in England and Wales: post-Carboniferous tectonics and stratigraphy.* WHITAKER, A (editor). 71pp. (Glasgow: Blackie.)

CHARLESWORTH, J K. 1929. The South Wales end-moraine. *Q. J. Geol. Soc. London*, Vol. 85, 335–358.

CHERNS, L. 1980. Hardgrounds in the Lower Leintwardine Beds (Silurian) of the Welsh Borderland. *Geol. Mag.*, Vol. 117, 311–326.

CLARKE, B B. 1934. The geomorphology of the lower Wye valley. Unpublished M.Sc. thesis, University of Birmingham.

— 1949. A glacial deposit at Byford. *Trans. Woolhope Nat. Field Club*, Vol. 32, 212–218.

— 1951. The geology of Garnons Hill and some observations on the formation of the Downtonian rocks of Herefordshire. *Trans. Woolhope Nat. Field Club*, Vol. 33, 97–111.

— 1952. The geology of Dinmore Hill, Herefordshire, with a description of a new Myriapod from the Dittonian rocks there. *Trans. Woolhope Nat. Field Club*, Vol. 33, 222–236.

— 1955a. The Old Red Sandstone of the Merbach Ridge, with an account of the Middlewood Sandstone, a new fossiliferous horizon 500 feet below the Psammosteus Limestone. *Trans. Woolhope Nat. Field Club*, Vol. 34, 195–218.

— 1955b. An occurrence of the basal Dittonian zone fossil at Derndale Hill. *Trans Woolhope Nat. Field Club*, Vol. 34, 273.

COCKS, L R M, HOLLAND, C H, RICKARDS, R B, and STRACHAN, I. 1971. A correlation of Silurian rocks in the British Isles. *Q. J. Geol. Soc. London*, Vol. 127, 103–136.

CROSS, P, and HODGSON, J M. 1975. New evidence for the glacial diversion of the River Teme near Ludlow, Salop. *Proc. Geol. Assoc.*, Vol. 86, 313–331.

CURLEY, T. 1858. *Map and geological sections of the City of Hereford compiled from the data of the parliamentary, trigonometrical, and detailed surveys made for improvement works.* (London: Hereford Improvement Committee.)

— 1863. On the gravels and other superficial deposits of Ludlow, Hereford and Skipton. *Q. J. Geol. Soc. London*, Vol. 19, 175–179.

— 1867a. Geological field address. *Trans Woolhope Nat. Field Club*, Vol. for 1866, 170–174.

— 1867b. On the occurrence of a local deposit of peat with shell marl at Hereford. *Trans. Woolhope Nat. Field Club*, Vol. for 1866, 253–254.

— 1887. Extinct animals and British fossil oxen discovered in Herefordshire. *Trans. Woolhope Nat. Field Club* (1880), Vol. for 1877–80, 248–251.

DAVISON, C. 1924. *A history of British earthquakes.* 416pp. (Cambridge: Cambridge University Press.)

— 1927. The Hereford earthquake of 15th August, 1926. *Geol. Mag.*, Vol. 64, 162–167.

DAWKINS, W B. 1869. On the distribution of the British post-glacial mammals. *Q. J. Geol. Soc. London*, Vol. 25, 192–217.

DEPARTMENT OF ENERGY. 1978. *UK land well records. Collington No. 1, Hereford.* (London: HMSO.)

DINES, H G, HOLLINGWORTH, S E, EDWARDS, W, BUCHAN, S. and WELCH, F B A. 1940. The mapping of Head deposits. *Geol. Mag.*, Vol. 77, 198–226.

DRURY, G H. 1954. Contribution to a general theory of meandering valleys. *Am. J. Sci.*, Vol. 252, 193–224.

DWERRYHOUSE, A R, and MILLER, A A. 1930. Glaciation of Clun Forest, Radnor Forest and some adjoining districts. *Q. J. Geol. Soc. London*, Vol. 86, 96–129.

FITCH, F J, and MILLER, J A. 1964. The age of the paroxysmal Variscan orogeny in England. *Q. J. Geol. Soc. London*, Vol. 120S, 159–173.

— — and WILLIAMS, S C. 1970. Isotopic ages of British Carboniferous rocks. *C. R. 6ᵉ Congr. Intern. Strat. Géol. Carbonif. Sheffield 1967*, Vol. 2, 771–789.

FRANCIS, E A. 1975. Glacial sediments: a selective review. 43–68 in *Ice ages ancient and modern.* WRIGHT, A E, and MOSELEY, F (editors). 320pp. (Liverpool: Seel House Press.)

GARDINER, C I. 1927. The Silurian inlier of Woolhope (Herefordshire). *Q. J. Geol. Soc. London*, Vol. 52, 195–220.

GEORGE, T N. 1974. The Cenozoic evolution of Wales. 341–371 in *The Upper Palaeozoic and post-palaeozoic rocks of Wales.* 425pp. (Cardiff: University of Wales Press.)

GRINDLEY, H E. 1905. Further notes on ice-action and on ancient drainage systems connected with the Wye Valley. *Trans. Woolhope Nat. Field Club* (1904), Vol. for 1902–4, 336–338.

— 1911. The glaciation of the Wye Valley. *Trans. Woolhope Nat. Field Club* (1905), Vol. for 1905–7, 160–167.

— 1918. The gravels of the basin of the lower Lugg and their relation to an earlier river system. *Trans. Woolhope Nat. Field Club* (1914). Vol. for 1914–1917, 227–230.

— 1921. The superficial deposits of the basin of the middle Wye. *Trans. Woolhope Nat. Field Club* (1918), Vol. for 1918–20, ii–vii.

— 1925. Observations on the Midland Drift as seen in two sandpits at Mathon. *Trans. Woolhope Nat. Field Club* (1923), Vol. for 1921–23, 176–177.

— 1954. The Wye Glacier. 36–47 in *Herefordshire, its natural history, archeology and history* (Centenary Volume of the Woolhope Nat. Field Club). 254pp. (Gloucester: British Publishing Co.)

HARDY, A R. 1972. Water Resources Act 1963. Section 14. Survey of water resources and demands. 42pp. (Hereford: The Wye River Authority.)

— and YOUNG, C P. 1973. Yazor Brook gravels investigation. (Investigations of superficial deposits in the Hereford area). Interim Report to 30 June, 1973. Wye River Authority. [Unpublished.]

— — 1975. Yazor Brook gravels investigation. (Investigations of superficial deposits in the Hereford area). Final Report (April, 1975). Wye River Authority. [Unpublished.]

HEY, R W. 1959. Pleistocene deposits on the west side of the Malvern Hills. Geol. Mag., Vol. 96, 403–417.

HODGSON, J M. 1972. Soils of the Ludlow District. Mem. Soil Surv. G.B., Engl. Wales. 139pp.

— and PALMER, R C. 1971. Soils in Herefordshire 1: sheet SO 53 (Hereford South). Soil Surv. Rec. No. 2.

HOLLAND, C H. 1985. Synchronology. Philos. Trans. R. Soc. London, Ser. B, Vol. 309, 11–27.

— 1986. Does the golden spike still glitter? J. Geol. Soc. London, Vol. 143, 3–21.

— and LAWSON, J D. 1963. Facies patterns in the Ludlow of Wales and the Welsh Borderland. Liverpool Manchester Geol. J., Vol. 3, 269–288.

— — and WALMSLEY, V G. 1959. A revised classification of the Ludlovian succession at Ludlow. Nature, London, Vol. 184, 1037–1039.

— — 1963. The Silurian rocks of the Ludlow District, Shropshire. Bull. Br. Mus. (Nat. Hist.) Geol., Vol. 8, 93–171.

— et al. 1978. A guide to stratigraphical procedure. Spec. Rep. Geol. Soc. London, No. 11. 18pp.

— LAWSON, J D, WALMSLEY, V G, and WHITE, D E. 1980. Ludlow stages. Lethaia, Vol. 13, 268.

JACKSON, J, and MUIR WOOD, R. 1980. The Earth flexes its muscles. New Sci., Vol. 88, 717–720.

JEFFREYS, H. 1927. On two British earthquakes. Monthly Notices R. Astron. Soc. Geophys. Suppl., Vol. 1, 483–493.

JUKES-BROWNE, A J. 1887. The geology of part of East Lincolnshire. Mem. Geol. Surv. G.B., Sheet 84.

KENDRICK, F M. 1979. Geology, 1979. Trans. Woolhope Nat. Field Club, Vol. 43, 77.

KING, W W. 1925. Notes on the 'Old Red Sandstone' of Shropshire. Proc. Geol. Assoc., Vol. 36, 383–389.

— 1934. The Downtonian and Dittonian strata of Great Britain and north-western Europe. Q. J. Geol. Soc. London, Vol. 90, 526–570.

KJELLESVIG-WAERING, E N. 1951. Downtonian (Silurian) Eurypterida from Perton, near Stoke Edith, Herefordshire. Geol. Mag., Vol. 88, 1–24.

LAWSON, J D. 1975. Ludlow benthonic assemblages. Palaeontology, Vol. 18, 509–525.

LEEDER, M R. 1975. Pedogenic carbonates and flood sediment accretion rates: a quantitative model for alluvial arid-zone lithofacies. Geol. Mag., Vol. 112, 257–270.

LILWALL, R C. 1976. Seismicity and seismic hazard in Britain. Seismological Bull., No. 4. 9pp. (London: HMSO for Institute of Geological Sciences.)

LIVERMORE, R A, SMITH, A G, and BRIDEN, J C. 1985. Palaeomagnetic constraints on the distribution of continents in the late Silurian and early Devonian. Philos. Trans. R. Soc. London, Ser. B, Vol. 309, 29–56.

LUCKMAN, B H. 1970. The Hereford Basin. 175–196 in The glaciations of Wales and adjoining regions. LEWIS, C A (editor). 378pp. (London: Longman.)

M'CULLOUGH, D M. 1869. The cornstones of Herefordshire and Monmouthshire. Trans. Woolhope Nat. Field Club, Vol. for 1868, 8–11.

MEREWETHER, F. 1871. On the drifts in the neighbourhood of Woolhope. Trans. Woolhope Nat. Field Club, Vol. for 1870, 173–177.

— 1887a. Geological drifts of the neighbourhood. Trans. Woolhope Nat. Field Club (1877), Vol. for 1877–80, 18–21.

— 1887b. Probable existence of an extensive lake that had at some time filled up the valleys of the Wye, Lugg, and Frome. Trans. Woolhope Nat. Field Club (1877), Vol. for 1877–80, 21–22.

MERRIMAN, R J. 1988. Mineralogy of the Townsend Tuff (Lower Old Red Sandstone) Herefordshire. Br. Geol. Surv. Tech. Rep., WG/88/11.

MOHAMAD, A H B. 1981. The petrology and depositional environment of the Upper Bringewood Beds of the south-eastern part of the Welsh Borderland. Unpublished PhD thesis, University of London.

MOORE, H C. 1905. Drifts in Herefordshire and evidences of action of land ice. Trans. Woolhope Nat. Field Club (1904), Vol. for 1902–4, 330–335.

MURCHISON, R I. 1833. On the sedimentary deposits which occupy the western parts of Shropshire and Herefordshire …(etc.). Proc. Geol. Soc. London, Vol. 1, 470–477. .

— 1834a. On the Old Red Sandstone in the counties of Hereford, Brecknock and Caemarthen …(etc.). Proc. Geol. Soc. London, Vol. 2, 11–13.

— 1834b. On the structure and classification of the Transition Rocks of Shropshire, Herefordshire and parts of Wales …(etc.). Proc. Geol. Soc. London, Vol. 2, 13–18.

— 1834c. On certain trap rocks in the counties of Salop, Montgomery, Radnor, Brecon, Caemarthen, Hereford, and Worcester; and the effects produced by them upon the stratified deposits. Proc. Geol. Soc. London, Vol. 2, 85–93.

— 1834d. On the gravel and alluvial deposits of those parts of the counties of Hereford, Salop and Worcester which consist of Old Red Sandstone with an account of the puffstone or travertin of Spouthouse, and of the Southstone Rock near Tenbury. Proc. Geol. Soc. London, Vol. 2, 77–78.

— 1835. The gravel and alluvia of S. Wales and Siluria as distinguished from a northern drift covering Lancashire, Cheshire, N. Salop, and parts of Worcester and Gloucester. Proc. Geol. Soc. London, Vol. 2, 230–236.

— 1839. The Silurian System, founded on geological researches in the counties of Salop, Hereford …(etc.). 768pp. (London: John Murray.)

— 1854. Siluria. 523pp. (London: John Murray.)

MUSSON, R M W, NEILSON, G, and BURTON, P W. 1984. Macroseismic reports on historical British earthquakes. VIII: South Wales. Rep. Global Seismol. Unit, Br. Geol. Surv., No. 233a and b. [Unpublished.]

OLDHAM, R D. 1926. Depth of origin of the earthquake of August 15th. Nature, London, Vol. 118, 302–303.

OWEN, T R. 1953. The structure of the Neath Disturbance between Bryniau Gleision and Glynneath, South Wales. Q. J. Geol. Soc. London, Vol. 109, 333–365.

— 1974. The Variscan Orogeny in Wales. 285–294 in The Upper Palaeozoic and post-Palaeozoic rocks of Wales. OWEN, T R (editor). 426pp. (Cardiff: University of Wales.)

— and WEAVER, J D. 1983. The structure of the main South Wales Coalfield and its margins. 74–87 in *The Variscan fold belt in the British Isles*. HANCOCK, P L (editor). 217pp. (Bristol: Hilger.)

PALMER, R C. 1972. *Soils in Herefordshire III: sheet SO 34 (Staunton-on-Wye). Soil Surv. Rec.* No. 11.

PARKER, A, ALLEN, J R L, and WILLIAMS, B P J. 1983. Clay mineral assemblages of the Townsend Tuff Bed (Lower Old Red Sandstone), South Wales and the Welsh Borders. *J. Geol. Soc.*, Vol. 140, 769–779.

PENN, I E. 1987. Geophysical logs in the stratigraphy of Wales and adjacent offshore and onshore areas. *Proc. Geol. Assoc.*, Vol. 98, 275–314.

PENNY, L F. 1974. Quaternary. 245–264 in *The geology and Mineral Resources of Yorkshire*. RAYNER, D H, and HEMINGWAY, J E (editors). 405pp. *Spec. Rep. Yorks. Geol. Soc.*

PHILLIPS, J. 1848. The Malvern Hills compared with the Palaeozoic district of Abberley ...(etc.). *Mem. Geol. Surv. G.B.*, Vol. 2.

PHIPPS, C B, and REEVE, F A E. 1967. Stratigraphy and geological history of the Malvern, Abberley and Ledbury hills. *Geol. J.*, Vol. 5, 339–368.

— — 1969. Structural geology of the Malvern, Abberley and Ledbury hills. *Q. J. Geol. Soc. London*, Vol. 125, 1–37.

POCOCK, R W. 1940. South Wales and Bristol District. 25–26 in *Summary of progress for 1938*. GEOLOGICAL SURVEY OF GREAT BRITAIN. (London: Her Majesty's Stationery Office.)

— and Whitehead, T H. 1935. *British regional geology: The Welsh Borderland*. (1st edition). (London: HMSO for Geological Survey G.B.)

POCOCK, T I. 1925. Terraces and drifts of the Welsh border and their relation to the drift of the English Midlands. *Z. Gletscherkd*, Vol. 13, 10–38.

— 1940. Glacial drift and river terraces of the Herefordshire Wye. *Z. Gletscherkd*, Vol. 27, 98–117.

PRICE, R J. 1973. *Glacial and fluvioglacial landforms. Geomorphology texts*. 242pp. (London: Longman.)

RAST, N. 1983. Variscan Orogeny. 1–19 in *The Variscan fold belt in the British Isles*. HANCOCK, P L (editor). 217pp. (Bristol: Hilger.)

READING, H G. 1980. Characteristics and recognition of strike-slip fault systems. *Spec. Publ. Int. Assoc. Sedimentol.*, Vol. 4, 7–26.

REED, F R C. 1934. Downtonian fossils from the Anglo-Welsh area. *Q. J. Geol. Soc. London*, Vol. 90, 571–585.

REYNOLDS, S H. 1908. The basic intrusion of Bartestree, near Hereford. *Q. J. Geol. Soc. London*, Vol. 64, 501–511.

RICHARDSON, L. 1911. An outline of the geology of Herefordshire. *Trans. Woolhope Nat. Field Club* (1905), Vol. for 1905–1907, 1–68.

— 1935. Wells and springs of Herefordshire. *Mem. Geol. Surv. G.B.*

ROSE, J. 1987. Status of the Wolstonian glaciation in the British Quaternary. *Quaternary Newsl.*, No. 53, 1–9.

SANDERSON, D J, and MARCHINI, W R D. 1984. Transpression. *J. Struct. Geol.*, Vol. 6, 449–458.

SCOBIE, M J. 1907. The geological report of the proceedings at the 1st excursion of the club. *Trans. Woolhope Nat. Field Club* (1852), Vol. for 1852–65, 14–17.

SHOTTON, F W. 1986. Glaciations in the United Kingdom. *Quaternary Sci. Rev.*, Vol. 5, 293–297.

SIMON, J B, and BLUCK, B J. 1982. Palaeodrainage of the southern margin of the Caledonian mountain chain in the northern British Isles. *Trans. R. Soc. Edinburgh, Earth Sci.*, Vol. 73, 11–15.

SMITH, A G, HURLEY, A M, and BRIDEN, J C. 1981. *Phanerozoic paleocontinental world maps*. 102pp. (Cambridge: Cambridge University Press.)

SMITH, D B. 1980. Ross-on-Wye Special 10 000 Sheet (Keyworth: British Geological Survey.)

SQUIRRELL, H C. 1973. The Downtonian–Dittonian boundary. *J. Geol. Soc. London*, Vol. 129, 205–206.

— and DOWNING, R A. 1969. Geology of the South Wales Coalfield, part 1, Newport (Mon.). *Mem. Geol. Surv. G.B.*, Sheet 249.

— and TUCKER, E V. 1960. The geology of the Woolhope inlier (Herefordshire). *Q. J. Geol. Soc. London*, Vol. 116, 139–185.

— — 1982. Woolhope and Gorsley. 9–17 *in* The Silurian inliers of the south-eastern Welsh Borderland. LAWSON, J D, CURTIS, M L K, SQUIRRELL, H C, TUCKER, E V, and WALMSLEY, V G. *Geol. Assoc. Guide*, No. 5. 33pp.

STAMP, L D. 1923. The base of the Devonian, with special reference to the Welsh Borderland. *Geol. Mag.*, Vol. 60, 367–372; 385–410.

STRICKLAND, H E. 1852. On the protruded mass of Upper Ludlow rock at Hagley Park in Herefordshire. *Q. J. Geol. Soc. London*, Vol. 8, 381–385.

— 1853. On the distribution and organic contents of the 'Ludlow Bone Bed' in the districts of Woolhope and May Hill. *Q. J. Geol. Soc. London*, Vol. 9, 8–12.

SUMBLER, M G, BRANDON, A. and GREGORY, D M. 1985. Grindley's Flood: a report of a marine clay in the Wye valley near Hereford. *Quaternary Newsl.*, No. 46, 18–25.

SUTCLIFFE, A J. 1985. *On the track of Ice Age mammals*. 224pp. (London: Br. Mus. (Nat. Hist.).)

SYMONDS, W S. 1861a. On the geology of the railway from Worcester to Hereford. *Edinburgh New Philos. J.*, Series 2, Vol. 13, 204–232.

— 1861b. On some phenomena connected with the drifts of the Severn, Avon, Wye and Usk. *Edinburgh New Philos. J.*, Series 2, Vol. 14, 281.

— 1867. *Notes on the geology of Herefordshire*. 20pp. (Hereford: Joseph Jones.)

— 1872. *Records of the rocks. (Or notes on the geology, natural history and antiquities of North and South Wales, Devon and Cornwall).* 433pp. (London: John Murray.)

— 1889. i–xxxvii in *A flora of Herefordshire*. PURCHAS, W H, and LEY, A (editors). 549pp. (Hereford: Jakeman and Carver.)

— 1907. The Old Red Sandstone of Herefordshire. *Trans. Woolhope Nat. Field Club* (1854), Vol. for 1852–65, 114–120.

TUCKER, E V. 1960. Ludlovian biotite-bearing bands. *Geol. Mag.*, 97, 245–249.

TUNBRIDGE, I P. 1983. Geophysical down-hole recognition of the Lower Devonian 'Psammosteus' Limestone and Townsend Tuff Bed, South Wales. *Geol. J.*, Vol. 18, 325–329.

WATKINS, R. 1979. Benthic community organization in the Ludlow Series of the Welsh Borderland. *Bull. Br. Mus. (Nat. Hist.) Geol.*, Vol. 31, 175–280.

WATSON, J. 1911. *British and foreign building stones.* 483pp. (Cambridge: University Press.)

WELCH, F B A, and TROTTER, F M. 1961. Geology of the country around Monmouth and Chepstow. *Mem. Geol. Surv. G.B.*, Sheets 233 and 250.

WEST. R G. 1968. *Pleistocene geology and biology.* 379pp. (London: Longmans.)

WHITE, E I. 1945. The genus *Phialaspis* and the '*Psammosteus* Limestones'. *Q. J. Geol. Soc. London*, Vol. 101, 207–242.

— 1950a. The vertebrate faunas of the Lower Old Red Sandstone of the Welsh Borders. *Bull. Br. Mus. (Nat. Hist.) Geol.*, Vol. 1, 51–67.

— 1950b. *Pteraspis leathensis* White. A Dittonian zone-fossil. *Bull. Br. Mus. (Nat. Hist.) Geol.*, Vol. 1, 69–89.

WHITEFIELD, W A D. 1971. Soils in Herefordshire II: sheet SO 52 (Ross-on-Wye west). *Soil Surv. Rec.*, No. 3.

WHITEHEAD, T H, and POCOCK, R W. 1947. Dudley and Bridgnorth. *Mem. Geol. Surv. G.B.*, Sheet 167.

WILCOX, R E, HARDING, T P, and SEELY, D R. 1973. Basic wrench tectonics. *Bull. Am. Assoc. Pet. Geol.*, Vol. 57, 74–96.

WILLIAMS, B P J. 1980. The Devonian (Old Red Sandstone) rocks of the Variscan Foreland. 57–63 in *United Kingdom. Introduction to general geology and guides to excursions 002, 055, 093 and 151. 26th International Geological Congress, Paris 1980.* OWEN, T R (editor). (London: Institute of Geological Sciences.)

WILLS, L J. 1937. The Pleistocene development of the Severn from Brignorth to the sea. *Q. J. Geol. Soc. London*, Vol. 94, 161–242.

— 1950. *The palaeogeography of the Midlands.* 147pp. (Liverpool: Liverpool University Press.)

WOODCOCK, N H. 1984a. Early Palaeozoic sedimentation and tectonics in Wales. *Proc. Geol. Assoc.*, Vol. 95, 323–335.

— 1984b. The Pontesford Lineament, Welsh Borderland. *J. Geol. Soc. London*, Vol. 141, 1001–1014.

WOODWARD, H. 1871. On a new species of *Eurypterus* (*E. brodiei*) from Perton, near Stoke Edith, Herefordshire. *Q. J. Geol. Soc. London*, Vol. 27, 261–263.

WORSLEY, P. 1977. Periglaciation. 205–219 in *British Quaternary Studies. Recent advances.* SHOTTON, F W (editor). 298pp. (Oxford: Clarendon Press.)

WORSSAM, B C, ELLISON, R A, and MOORLOCK, B S P. *In press.* Geology of the country around Tewkesbury. *Mem. Geol. Surv. G.B.*, Sheet 216.

ZIEGLER, P A. 1982. *Geological atlas of Western and Central Europe.* 120pp. (The Hague: Shell International Petroleum.)

# APPENDIX

## List of Geological Survey photographs

Copies of these colour photographs may be seen in the Library of the British Geological Survey, Keyworth, Nottingham NG12 5GG. Colour and black and white prints and 35 mm colour slides may be bought. National Grid references, all in 100 km square SO, are those of the view points. The photographs belong to Series A.

### LUDLOW

13872 The Shucknall Anticline in the Lower Ludlow Siltstone Formation, Shucknall Hill Quarry [5914 4305] (Plate 1)

13873–5 Lower Ludlow Siltstone Formation, Shucknall Hill Quarry, Shucknall Hill [5914 4305]

13876–7 Upper Ludlow Siltstone Formation (Upper Bodenham Beds) in a small disused quarry (now a garden) at Shucknall [5871 4264] (13877 Plate 2)

13878 Shucknall Hill from the south at Stoke Edith [602 403]

13882–3 Aymestry Limestone in the backscarp of The Slip, Dormington [5927 3980]

13884–5, 13887 Aymestry Limestone and lower part of the Upper Ludlow Siltstone Formation, Perton Quarry [5955 3995]

13886 Aymestry Limestone, Perton Quarry [5955 3995]

13888 Upper Ludlow Siltstone Formation (Upper Perton Beds), small disused quarry, Stoke Edith [6036 4043]

(See also 13879–81)

### LOWER OLD RED SANDSTONE

13300 Raglan Mudstone at Wye Cliffe, Breinton, Hereford [4605 3945]

13870–1 Withington Church, built of a local coarse-grained sandstone in the Raglan Mudstone [5657 4347]

13879 The Rushall Formation conformably overlying Upper Ludlow Siltstone, Perton Lane Quarry, Perton [5971 4035]

13940 Adit mine in Bishop's Frome Limestone, Credenhill [4459 4485]

13941 The Bishop's Frome Limestone in a shallow adit mine; Credenhill [4459 4485] (Plate 3)

13942 Entrance to the adit mine in the Bishop's Frome Limestone on Credenhill [4459 4485] (Plate 4)

13943 'Colour banding' and cross-stratification in the lowest sandstone of the St Maughans Formation, Credenhill [4459 4485]

13946 Lower part of the Bishop's Frome Limestone, Marlbrook limepits, Newton [5056 5461]

13954 Parallel laminated sandstone, St Maughans Formation, exposed in a quarry on Wormsley Hill [4211 4863]

13955 Cross-stratified sandstone, St Maughans Formation, exposed in a quarry on Wormsley Hill [4211 4863]

13956–7 Uppermost part of Raglan Mudstone exposed in a forestry track, Nupton [4460 4811]

13958 Bishop's Frome Limestone, forestry track, Nupton Hill [4453 4814]

13959 Butthouse Knapp, a conical hill capped by St Maughans Formation [4306 4789]

13960 Pyon Hill, a conical hill capped by the Bishop's Frome Limestone [435 513]

13961 General view from Dilwyn looking southwards towards Burton and Wormsley hills which are capped by St Maughans Formation [412 543]

13966 Bishop's Frome Limestone escarpment, Bishop's Frome [638 484]

13967 Intraformational conglomerate at Instone Court Quarry, Bishop's Frome [6554 4991]

14161 Dessication crack casts on the sole of a sandstone in the St Maughans Formation [5910 5788] (Plate 6)

14164–66 St Maughans Formation in a small disused quarry, Pencombe, showing low angle planar cross-bedded sandstone and intraformational conglomerate sets which are internally parallel and low angle cross-laminated [5765 5339] (14165 Plate 5)

14167 Parallel-bedded sandstones, St Maughans Formation, Birley Hill Quarry [4575 5222]

14168 Sandstone and pedogenic limestone, St Maughans Formation, Birley Hill Quarry [4569 5213]

14169 Bishop's Frome Limestone, Brierley Wood [4980 5548]

14175 Waterfall formed by St Maughans Formation sandstone, Little Cowarne [6001 5128]

14230 The wooded escarpment of the St Maughans Formation, Queens Wood, Dinmore Hill [505 506]

(See also 13878 and 13890)

### CARBONIFEROUS INTRUSION

13867–9 The dolerite-basalt intrusion and hornfelsed country rock at Lowe's Hill Quarry, Bartestree [5663 4045]

### QUATERNARY: OLDER DRIFT

13287 Older Fluvioglacial Terrace Deposits (lower gravels) in the Upper Lyde Pit, Burghill–Portway [4925 4472] (Plate 7)

13289 Slumped beds of Older Fluvioglacial Terrace Deposits (upper gravels and median sands and silts) in the eastern Burghill Pit, Burghill [4822 4512]

13290 Cemented lens in the upper gravels of the Older Fluvioglacial Terrace Deposits, western Burghill Pit, Burghill [4805 4522]

13293 Till of the Newer Drift terminal moraine overlying the lower gravels of the Older Fluvioglacial Terrace Deposits (lower gravels), Burlton Court Pit, Burghill [4849 4414]

13294 Detail of the contact of till of the Newer Drift terminal moraine on the lower gravels of the Older Fluvioglacial Terrace Deposits, Burlton Court Gravel Pit, Burghill [4849 4417]

13295 Till of the Newer Drift terminal moraine resting on the lower gravels of the Older Fluvioglacial Terrace Deposits, Burlton Court Pit, Burghill [4849 4415]

13891–2 Slumped, partly vertical, ill-sorted gravels, Older Fluvioglacial Terrace Deposits, Sutton Hill Pit [5408 4640]

13893   Slumped, ill-sorted gravels, Older Fluvioglacial Terrace Deposits, Sutton Hill Pit [5407 4645]

13894–5   Slumped and folded Older Fluvioglacial Terrace Deposits, Sutton Hill Pit [5418 4637]

13896   Immature, ill-sorted, coarse, partly cryoturbated gravel of the Older Fluvioglacial Terrace Deposits, Norton Court Pit, Marden [5379 4956]

13947–9   Ill-sorted deltaic gravels probably of the Older Fluvioglacial Terrace Deposits, Blackwardine railway cutting, Stoke Prior [5300 5660]

13950   Ill-sorted gravels of the Older Fluvioglacial Terrace Deposits in a small gravel pit at Risbury Bridge [5395 5496]

13963   Ill-sorted gravels of the Older Fluvioglacial Terrace Deposits, gravel pit, Stoke Lacy [6223 4842]

13964   Well-stratified fine gravel of the Older Fluvioglacial Terrace Deposits, gravel pit, Windmill Hill [6063 4870]

13965   Well-stratified fine gravel overlying coarse ill-sorted unstratified gravel, Older Fluvioglacial Terrace Deposits, gravel pit, Windmill Hill [6063 4870]

14158–60   Older Fluvioglacial Terrace Deposits, gravel pit, Pudleston [5637 5904]

14162   Cemented lenses of gravel, Older Fluvioglacial Terrace Deposits, gravel pit near Gilhorn Cottage, Court Hill [5220 5571]

14163   Ill-sorted gravels, with sand lens, of the Older Fluvioglacial Terrace Deposits, gravel pit near Stirbridge Cottages, Court Hill [5547 5598]

14171   Ill-sorted coarse gravels of the Older Fluvioglacial Terrace Deposits, gravel pit at Ryelands Croft, Leominster [4906 5831]

14172–4   Slumped gravel, sand and silt beds of the Older Fluvioglacial Terrace Deposits at Crick's Green gravel pit [6273 5160]

14224   Poorly sorted gravels of the Older Fluvioglacial Terrace Deposits in a small gravel pit west of Blackwardine, Stoke Prior [5267 5673]

14225–6   Imbricated gravels of the Older Fluvioglacial Terrace Deposits in a small gravel pit south of Blackwardine School, Stoke Prior [5278 5646]

14227   Small faults in gravels of the Older Fluvioglacial Terrace Deposits in a small gravel pit south of Blackwardine School, Stoke Prior [5278 5646]

14229   Cemented, coarse, ill-sorted gravel of the Older Fluvioglacial Terrace Deposits, Risbury [5421 5494]

(See also 13962)

## QUATERNARY: NEWER DRIFT

13291   Anticlinal fold in slumped ill-sorted gravels of the kettle-kame moraine, gravel pit, Stretton Sugwas [4562 4217]

13299, 13301   Slumped laminated silts and tills in kettle-kame moraine, Stretton Sugwas gravel pits [4573 4222] (13299 Plate 8)

13937   Kettle hole in kettle-kame moraine, Canon Bridge [427 402]

13938   Kettle hole in kettle-kame moraine, Canon Bridge [434 407]

13962   Well-stratified fine gravels overlain by poorly stratified ill-sorted gravels, Glacial Sand and Gravel, gravel pit, Stretford [4393 5618]

14170   Poorly sorted gravel of the Glacial Sand and Gravel exposed in a pit at Ivington Bury [4747 5686]

14215   Flat-lying to cross-bedded ill-sorted gravel overlying poorly laminated silty sand, Fluvioglacial Terrace Deposits, Stretton Sugwas [4472 4228]

14216–7   Cross-bedded ill-sorted gravel overlying poorly laminated silty sand, Fluvioglacial Terrace Deposits, Stretton Sugwas [4477 4220]

14218   Flat-lying sand of the Fluvioglacial Terrace Deposits with a sharp contact on gently inclined, slumped, coarse, ill-sorted gravels of the kettle-kame moraine, Stretton Sugwas gravel pits [4517 4254]

14219   Poorly sorted immature gravel with a thin laminated silt bed affected by a monoclinal flexure, kettle-kame moraine, Stretton Sugwas gravel pits [448 424]

14220–3   A recumbent isoclinal fold in ill-sorted poorly bedded gravels of the kettle-kame moraine, Stretton Sugwas gravel pits [4485 4237]

14228   The Devensian terminal moraine across the Stretford Brook valley east of Leominster [530 582]

(See also 13293–5 and 13951–3)

## QUATERNARY: ALLUVIUM, TERRACE DEPOSITS AND LANDSLIP

13292   Alluvium of Yazor Brook overlying cryoturbated fluvioglacial gravel [4506 4231]

13880   The Slip, Dormington and a view northwards across the Frome valley to Shucknall Hill and beyond [5926 3980] (Frontispiece)

13881   The Slip, Dormington, from below looking south [5918 4005]

13889   Imbricated, well-sorted, mature gravel of the Sutton Walls Terrace, Sutton Walls [5235 4635]

13890   Gravel of the Sutton Walls Terrace overlying blocky siltstone of the Raglan Mudstone, road cutting, Sutton Walls [5235 4635]

13944–5   Landslips in kettle-kame moraine along the River Wye, Bridge Sollers [415 419]

13951–3   Fluvial gravels of the River Lugg overlying fluvioglacial gravels, Bodenham gravel pit [5183 5123]

# INDEX

**BRITISH GEOLOGICAL SURVEY**

Keyworth, Nottingham NG12 5GG
Plumtree (060 77) 6111

Murchison House, West Mains Road,
Edinburgh EH9 3LA      031-667 1000

London Information Office, Geological Museum
Exhibition Road, London SW7 2DE
01-589 4090

The full range of Survey publications is available
through the Sales Desks at Keyworth and
Murchison House, Edinburgh. Selected items can
be bought at the BGS London Information Office
and orders are accepted here for all publications.
The adjacent Geological Museum bookshop stocks
the more popular books for sale over the counter.
Most BGS books and reports are listed in
HMSO's Sectional List 45, and can be bought
from HMSO and through HMSO agents and
retailers. Maps are listed in the BGS Map
Catalogue and the Ordnance Survey's Trade
Catalogue, and can be bought from Ordnance
Survey agents as well as from BGS.

*The British Geological Survey carries out the geological*
*survey of Great Britain and Northern Ireland (the latter*
*an agency service for the government of Northern Ireland)*
*and of the surrounding continental shelf, as well as its*
*basic research projects. It also undertakes programmes of*
*British technical aid in geology in developing countries as*
*arranged by the Overseas Development Administration.*

*The British Geological Survey is a component body of the*
*Natural Environment Research Council.*

Maps and diagrams in this book use topography
based on Ordnance Survey mapping

**HER MAJESTY'S STATIONERY OFFICE**

HMSO publications are available from:

**HMSO Publications Centre**
(Mail and telephone orders)
PO Box 276, London SW8 5DT
Telephone orders 01-873 9090
General enquiries 01-873 0011
*Queueing system in operation for both numbers*

**HMSO Bookshops**
49 High Holborn, London WC1V 6HB
  01-873 0011 (Counter service only)
258 Broad Street, Birmingham B1 2HE
  021-643 3740
Southey House, 33 Wine Street, Bristol BS1 2BQ
  (0272) 264306
9 Princess Street, Manchester M60 8AS
  061-834 7201
80 Chichester Street, Belfast BT1 4JY
  (0232) 238451
71 Lothian Road, Edinburgh EH3 9AZ
  031-228 4181

**HMSO's Accredited Agents**
(see Yellow Pages)

*And through good booksellers*